Original Title: *Futurismi*

First published in Milan in 2016 by Ulrico Hoepli Editore S.p.A.
under the title *Futurismi*.
Revised edition with English translation by Michael Friel, first published 2018.

Typesetting: Corpo4 Team, Milano

EGEA S.p.A.
Via Salasco, 5 - 20136 Milano
Tel. 02/5836.5751 – Fax 02/5836.5753
egea.edizioni@unibocconi.it – www.egeaeditore.it

ISBN Domestic Edition   978-88-99902-33-9
ISBN International Edition   978-88-85486-68-3
ISBN Moby pocket Edition   978-88-85486-69-0
ISBN Epub Edition   978-88-85486-70-6

First edition: November 2018

Table of Contents

To Chiara, Valeria, Luca, Jacopo, Giorgio, Matilde

Introduction

Tourism as we understand it today, with vast numbers of people on the move, began towards the middle of the twentieth century. Only a few countries were involved, ones that were fortunate in terms of geographical position and natural and artistic beauty; virtually all of them, including Italy of course, were bathed by the Mediterranean.

Tourism in those days was called *"going on holiday"* and tourists were *"holiday-makers"*. For those who could afford them, holidays were often taken in the same place year after year, and perhaps for three or four weeks consecutively, i.e. for the whole time that it was possible to get away from home and the workplace. These were *the* holidays.

Where tourism existed it flourished and thrived on monopolistic factors, with numbers in continuous growth and easy to plan for. Holiday-makers had simple requirements that were easy to satisfy and investments guaranteed secure yields in a context that was still unburdened by excessive regulation.

The sea held sway with a season that lasted less than four months per year, but which was still often enough to guarantee a good income for the entire year. Tourists flooded in, particular into the Mediterranean, especially from Great Britain, Germany and then the other European countries and the United States. There were few others nationalities, almost exceptions. Travelling, especially far away, was not easy and was quite expensive.

And so the most common means of transport was the car, followed closely by the train. In many countries, and in some more than others, tourism was still not seen as a real economic sector; few people bothered with it and it essentially centred on the hotel industry.

Sixty years have passed since then and the situation has changed radically. Thanks to the progress made in the transport sector it has become possible for almost every country in the world to engage in tourism after realising that it is an economic sector that can provide extraordinary opportunities for growth, with the creation of revenue and jobs.

Today tourism is recognised as one of the most promising *capital saving and labour intensive* sectors of the world economy; one that is growing and that will continue to grow more for many years at steady rates. Several factors contribute towards the formulation of these rosy forecasts and these unquestionably include higher world population, the constant growth of the average per capita income and, obviously, the benefits offered by a vigorous global competitive framework that is growing exponentially.

In addition to this is another extremely important component: travellers' behaviour has changed radically in recent decades, especially since 2000.

Today the trip, the holiday, the break from everyday routine, and the desire to discover and get to know new places and other worlds, have become much more important than they were just a few years ago and have been climbing step by step up the ladder of our priorities.

The tourism of the past when operators' success was guaranteed and linked to the shrewd foresight of an eager entrepreneurial class is a distant memory. Today, in a much more dynamic, articulated, changeable and highly competitive environment, nothing can be left to chance and to spontaneity. What dominates in travelling and holidaying nowadays are the search for knowledge, satisfying one's curiosity and desires and living different experiences, for weekend breaks or for longer periods, and but ones that are scattered over the entire year.

The sea, the mountains and cultural centres the cities of art have gradually been joined by hundreds of new destinations all over the world, located outside the traditional tourist circuits. Thanks to traditions, fiestas, events, and local tangible and intangible products and distinctions, any place can become an interesting tourist destination. As a result, designing new tourist products and planning for them is taking on innovative contours that respond adequately to the new demand generated by increasingly informed and demanding tourists who make decisions quickly and are attentive to the environment and its sustainability.

Tourism has therefore become a highly complex and multifaceted sector that calls for new skills and roles and, above all, for the involvement of lots of new actors: no longer the old vertical supply chain with a hotel at the centre and a few services around it. Today, partnering and collaboration and the networks associated with them have become horizontal and transversal; they expand and interweave even with areas that are seemingly distinct and distant from tourism, but which, taken as a whole, are capable of creating high-content synergies, generating interest and becoming identities. They are therefore capable of transforming themselves into a tourist product.

We have been accustomed, for many years, to pigeonholing tourism into categories such as seaside, mountain, spa, cities of art, religious, business, sport and so on, i.e. on the basis of the traveller primary interests.

Today, however, these subdivisions can seem insufficient for an adequate representation of the real situation. The interaction between tourist attractors, on the one hand and, on the other, sectors such as farming or culture in the broadest sense – those that are open to the contemporary, to music, design, fashion and big events – has become an essential and indispensable component of the tourist experience. The result is a complex picture and, in reality, an enrichment that has also contributed to radically modifying tourist consumption in the present day.

Today's tourists, with their new categories and clusters of millennials or of grey-haired globetrotters, have quite different rhythms, curiosities and interests than they did in the past, and these have a crucial effect on the variables in the dynamics of the tourist business such as seasonality: length of stay, booking times, where to eat, what to see and what to buy. All of this is obviously the result of developments in ICT and in the computerisation of tourism which have opened up paths that will take us a long way towards destinations that we can only imagine at present.

Everything has become easier, more immediate, available and cheaper for tourists. Tourist guides and maps have become obsolete, or niche products at best. We can get all the information we need from the Internet, social media and apps available today, whether it is a question of finding the nearest petrol station, museum opening times, restaurant menus, the price of a bottle of wine or the opinion of someone who has bought and drunk it. Everything is easy and within arm's reach. Technology and its tools have invaded our lives, in a certain sense imposing on us their languages, rhythms and rules to which we have become accustomed and adapted.

In a context like this one, of new tourists, new destinations, new products and new business models, tourism proposals that are promoted and marketed along traditional lines no longer have any sense and cannot find any space.

So what will happen in the coming years? Technological progress and the economic development of new areas of the world will unquestionably feed the expansion and sweeping transformation of tourism for as long as this is not thwarted by international political instability. New markets will open up and the current ones will be consolidated, we will dialogue in real time with our hotel or with our Airbnb guests using increasingly sophisticated smart devices, we will cruise on bigger and bigger ships and travel on faster and faster trains and many of us even by bike. But who will we be, where will we go, and what will we want to do? And how will tourism enterprises have to respond to these changes? How will we guarantee the sustainability of this enormous development of tourism? This is what this book wishes to unfold.

Acknowledgments

Despite being a short booklet, writing it was a great opportunity for us to exchange ideas with friends and colleagues, and to interact with some industry experts who have provided us with data and ideas. Our thanks go to them:

Alessandro Tommasi; Alain Dupeyras; Vittorio Netti; Massimo Temporelli; Elisa Pucci; Paola Borrione and the colleagues from the Santagata Foundation; Federica Olivares; Massimiliano De Martin; Marco Lombardi; Federico Capeci; Carlo Tursi; Fondazione CUOA; Andrea Sommariva.

1   2012: the Year of Tourist No. 1,000,000,000

In 2012 the United Nations World Tourism Organization (UNWTO) announced that if the growth rates of international arrivals were to remain at current levels, the 1 billion traveller mark would have been passed by the end of that year. And so it was: this milestone was reached on 13 December 2012 and the year closed at the end of that month with 1.035 billion international tourists around the world. This was an exceptional achievement, for at least two reasons: because it meant that on average one person in seven travelled beyond the borders of their country in 2012 (whether for business of pleasure is not important) and because tourism flows had increased 260% in the 30 years since 1982. Moreover, these growth rates only referred to outbound tourism flows and therefore did not consider all the tourism generated by a country's residents within its own national borders: for many countries this represents over 50% of the total.

Growth is therefore impressive for a sector of the *old economy* that has always existed; at least from the days of the Grand Tour onwards. Yet tourism has maintained its growth in a constant manner year after year despite the occasional backslide due to world crises such as the Gulf War, the Twin Towers Attack, the SARS epidemic or the 2008 financial crisis.

The 2018 forecasts tell us that this trend will continue at least until 2030, the year in which it is predicted to hit a figure of 1,800 billion international arrivals. Today these numbers make tourism one of the most interesting sectors of all, also thanks to its pervasive and transversal effects on the local economies and its ability to generate employment. And, given the low barriers of entry into the market, this is true for any country: potentially any location with a minimum of attractions and the ability to structure and promote a product can, in fact, compete to attract tourists.

Figure 1   International arrivals around the world (tourist arrivals received, million)

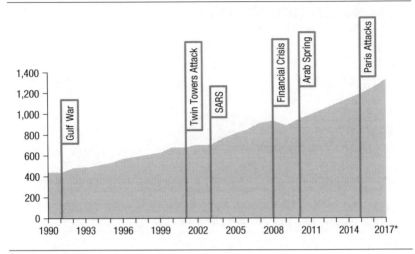

* provisional data
Source: Elaboration from UNWTO 2018 data

How did we get to this point? What has changed in tourism today since the days in the last century when fathers took the whole family to a holiday resort for the summer and came back to the city to work as was the case in the famous film, *The Seven Year Itch*.

It is interesting to recall the fundamental stages in this evolution as they allow us to admire the variety of factors that permitted the development of contemporary tourism – from technological innovation to progress in transportation, from international political stability to improved health safeguards – and also the variety of people and businesses that have contributed to the story.

So, just as we reconsider the way our lives have changed over the years, from clunky phones with rotary dials to the mobile and smartphone, it is worth recalling a few fundamental figures behind the transformation of people from travellers into tourists and who contributed to building an economy which was worth 7.2 trillion dollars in 2016: about 10% of global GNP and employing over 280 million people.

1845. An iconic year in history of tourism: this was when the British evangelist and entrepreneur Thomas Cook (1808–1892) opened the first travel agency in London. The development of the railways in Britain in 1830s

Table 1   The scale of global tourism

10% of World's GDP (direct, indirect, induced)
118 million people directly employed in the sector
1,323 million International Tourist Arrivals
1,340 billion International Tourism Receipts

Source: UNWTO and WTTC, 2018, data 2017

had made it possible for a growing number of working class people to take daytrips to the seaside or city for just a few shillings. Various associations had already been organised for such trips away from home by train. What set Thomas Cook apart, however, was that he engineered the product: in 1844 he entered into an agreement with Midland Counties Railways for the organisation of train excursions. Then, the following year, he founded his first agency and in just a few years expanded its activity abroad, in particular towards Italy and France, and especially for the 1855 Universal Exposition in Paris.

Cook's gravestone in Leicester reads:

Pioneer of travel. Founder of the world's largest travel organization.
First excursion Leicester to Loughborough 1841. Round the world 1872.
He brought travel to the millions.

He brought tourism to the masses. Over the years the group he created became one of the colossi of international tourism with annual revenues in 2017 of €8 billion and boosting 20 million clients.

1872. The Compagnie Internazionale des Wagons-Lits et du Tourisme was founded in Brussels, the main shareholder being the king, Leopold II (1835–1909). This was a firm for managing luxury railway services in the sleeper, catering and saloon car sector, which became fully operational in 1876 when the first sleeper cars in Europe came into service (they had already existed in the United States since 1859) and allowed passengers to travel while asleep as the advertisements of the time announced.

Then 1883 saw the start of service of the Orient Express, the world's first luxury tourism train and one year later the Compagnie Internationale des Wagons-Lits founded the Compagnie Internationale des Grands Hôtels, the first chain of luxury hotels in major cities. The first hotels

included Hôtel Terminus in Bordeaux and the Pera Palace Hôtel in Istan-
bul, built in 1892 for passengers travelling on the Orient Express, Hôtel
de la Plage in Ostend, Belgium, and the Grand Hôtel des Wagon-Lits in
Beijing.

1901. In the UK, Thomas Hiram Holding (1844–1930), a tailor of hum-
ble origin, founded Association of Cycle Campers, then the Camping and
Caravanning Club. Holding, an enthusiastic traveller, had decided to visit
the Scottish Highlands, combining stretches by canoe and nights in a tent.
Then during later trips in Connemara in Ireland he not only took his tent
but also his bicycle.

It was from these first excursions that the idea of camping was born.
In 1906 the Association of Cycle Campers opened in the first campsite
at Weybridge in Surrey and, in 1908, Holding wrote *The Camper's Hand-
book*, a practical guide to camping, which became a rapid success. The
birth of the Association of Cycle Campers was followed by the establishment of many other groups scattered across Europe such as the Camping
Club de Belgique (1912) and, in Italy, the ACCP (Auto Campeggio Club
Piemonte).

1919. Conrad Hilton (1887–1979) purchased his first hotel, the Mobley
Hotel in Cisco, Texas, in partnership with his father, Albert, a New Mexico businessman. Thanks to his business acumen, in just a few years Hilton
built the first hotel bearing his name, in Dallas, and began his unstoppable
rise which survived the Great Depression and the Second World War. It
led him to completely transform the hospitality world and create one of the
world's greatest hotel businesses, with over 4,600 resorts and timeshare
structures, and more than 758,000 rooms in 100 countries.

In 1947 the Roosevelt Hilton in New York was the first hotel in the
world to install TV sets in its guest rooms and Conrad Hilton was the
first hotel entrepreneur to grace the cover of *Time* magazine (in 1949 and
again in 1963).

1927. The Italian Labour Charter established an "annual paid holiday rest
period". Workers' rights and paid holidays were behind the development
of mass tourism, along with the rise in disposable income.

The country that first conceived a paid holiday period extended to all
workers was France in 1925 (in the UK the 1871 Bank Holiday Act only

referred to part of the population), but it was not until 1936 that the law was promulgated by the Front Populaire.

It was Italy, however, that in 1927 extended the right to paid rest days to the entire population. The Italian Constitution (Art. 36) later extended the inalienable right to holidays to every worker.

1949. The New York businessman, Frank X. McNamara, head of the American Hamilton Credit Corporation, invented a card for the credit payment of a series of accredited New York restaurants and hotels. Initially the little rectangular Diners' Card, as it was called, was not a great success and it was necessary to wait until the mid-1970s before the credit card began to catch on, also thanks to the arrival of VISA and Mastercard.

Though the credit card is clearly not a tourist invention, its introduction considerably facilitated international travel and progressively replaced *traveller's cheques*. These cheques, which could be purchased from banks and other financial institutions, allowed tourists to carry the sums of money they required for their trips without worrying that their cash could be lost or stolen, and were widespread all over the world until the middle of the 1990s.

Figure 2   Club Med Card 1957

Source: Wikimedia

1950. The first posters appeared in Paris announcing:

> For 15,000 Francs: Vacation in the Balearic Islands with Club Méditerranée... a new and friendly vacation program, a comfortable tent village, the most beautiful sites in the Mediterranean, a large and devoted staff, all Mediterranean sports, fast and comfortable journey, quality entertainment.[1]

To the surprise of the man who had made the offer, Gérard Blitz (1912–1990), a Belgian entrepreneur and water polo player, 2,400 people signed up, attracted by the idea of two weeks all-in in Majorca, playing sports and dancing on the beach, and enjoying convivial moments with good Mediterranean food and wine. In reality, the offer consisted of 36-hour trip by train and ship and the accommodation consisted of surplus American army tents. Nevertheless it was a great success and the beginning of the glorious story of Club Med and of holiday villages.

1955. In parallel with the development of the first holiday villages in the Mediterranean, a new leisure concept – destined for unstoppable global success – appeared in the United States in the mid-1950s: the theme park.

"It all started when my daughters were very young, and I took them to amusement parks on Sunday. I sat on a bench eating peanuts and looking around me. I said to myself, dammit, why can't there be a better place to take your children, where you can have fun together?"[2]

And so Walt Disney (1901–1966) invented that "better place" and called it Disneyland. It open its gates on 17 July 1955, in Anaheim, California, welcoming the first visitors to a magical world made not only of fairy tales and cartoon characters, but also incorporating an advanced reception and hospitality culture, founded on enormous research and technological innovation. Today, the top 25 theme parks in the world attract over 220 million people each year with annual visitor growth rates of over 4%. The Walt Disney Attractions group is the absolute market leader with over 134 million visitors in its ten main parks, scattered over three continents.

1972. An American ship-owner, Ted Arison (1924–1999), founded Carnival. This company revolutionised the cruise sector, sweeping away its elitist aura with *fun ships* fitted with every comfort and form of entertainment, and designed for a vast public of all classes and ages. Starting from its first ship, the *Mardi Gras*, Carnival began its ascent to become the top cruise company in the world at the start of the 1980s, in a market enjoying continuous growth: in 1989 Carnival purchased the Holland America Line, in 1992 the Seaborn Cruise Line, in 1997 Costa Crociere, the leader in the European cruise market and then, in 1998, the Cunard Line. In 2003, after negotiations with the antitrust authorities of the European Union, Carnival also took control of Princess Cruises. Today Carnival has a fleet of over 100 ships, over 120,000 employees worldwide, and revenues

Figure 3   The cruise ship *Mardi Gras* moored at Montreal on 28 August, 1979

Source: Wikimedia

of $17.5 billion (2017). In 2016, following the opening of diplomatic relations between Washington and Havana, the *Adonia* became to first cruise ship to dock in Cuba for almost 60 years.

1975. The World Tourism Organisation (WTO) was founded in Madrid. The UNWTO as it is today (it was transformed into a specialised United Nations agency in 2003) promotes tourism with a view to contributing to economic growth, to international relations, to peace, to the war on poverty, to universal respect and to the observance of human rights and fundamental liberties without distinctions of race, sex, language or religion. The agency collects and publishes the international statistics for the sector and works to identify new tourist destinations in order to ensure balanced distribution of tourist flows and encourage the economic and social growth of developing countries.

1987. Northwest Airlines 747 pilot and avid home workshop tinkerer, Robert Plath, devised a system for pulling a suitcase in an upright position by affixing a long handle and two wheels. And so the Rollaboard was born: originally conceived for the convenience of crews it soon became the rage in airport corridors and grabbed the attention and immense market of passengers. An early model of a case with wheels was patented in 1970 by Bernard D. Sadow, the manager of a Massachusetts company that produced luggage and overcoats, but it was not very functional as the case remained in a horizontal position. Such was the success of Plath's invention that he was able to give up flying and establish the company, Travelpro. In just a few years airlines were forced to change the structure of their planes and spend millions of dollars ($65 million for American Airlines and Continental alone) to adapt the overhead lockers for the new form of luggage, and airport designers had to envisage new travellators that could support the wheels of the cases, as well as trolley-size metal detectors.

1989. The Berlin Wall came down on 9 November. This event marked a pivotal moment in twentieth-century history not only from the political, social and economic standpoint but also for tourism. Free circulation between the two Germanies first of all, and then the progressive disappearance of the Soviet Bloc with the end of the Cold War, opened the way to reunification of one of the main destinations worldwide, made Europe and the world accessible to millions of tourists from the ex-socialist countries and triggered the development of tourism in the countries of Eastern Europe. By 2016 Germany was one of the main tourism players at global level with over 33 million international arrivals, highly developed domestic and outgoing tourism and a premier-league tourism industry: just think of TUI, the multinational colossus based in Hannover. Russia and the countries of the ex-USSR, on the other hand, are among the main tourism markets for Italy and many other tourism destinations, also in terms of growth rates.

1991. Ryanair had already been founded in 1985 by the Irish businessman, Tony Ryan. However it was from 1991 that the company as we know it today began its development, i.e. when the manager, Michael O'Leary, was charged with relaunching it. Using the no-frills approach of the American company Southwest Airlines as his inspiration, O'Leary adopted a new and highly aggressive strategy – based on essential services and low costs – to erode the European legacy airline market. Low prices were possible thanks to the savings made in the in-flight and ground services, which are generally provided by other full-service companies (airport lounge, catering, in-flight entertainment, frequent flyer plans, etc.), and to the use of a direct Internet sales channel, radical outsourcing policies, and secondary airports on the look-out for development opportunities that could offer Ryanair advantageous tariffs for airport services.

1996. Booking.com was founded in Holland and soon became world leader in the online bookings sector. This portal changed the world of tourism distribution forever, not simply in terms of the number of structures available but also because it allowed users to choose the solutions at the best guaranteed price (with rate parity clause) starting from the quality rating attributed to the hotels by the previous users.

Over 1.5 million nights are booked on Booking.com every day and the website – available in over 40 languages – offers 28,995,517 total reported listings, covering 140,419 destinations in 230 countries.

2000. Stephen Kaufer was aged 37 and wanted to organise a trip to Mexico. Unhappy with the glossy travel agency brochures, and with the intention of reducing the uncertainties in the quality of holidays, he designed a system for obtaining reliable information on destinations and services. And so TripAdvisor, a website dedicated to user-generated travel advice and linked to booking tools, was established in an office over a pizza takeaway in Newton, Massachusetts. Fifteen years later, TripAdvisor-branded sites (23 in all) constituted the largest community of travellers in the world with 456 million unique visitors every month, and over 660 million reviews and opinions on 7.7 million accommodation providers, restaurants and attractions. The sites operate in 49 countries and in 28 languages, and TripAdvisor employs 3,000 people around the world.

2016. An important if peripheral role is being played in the development of tourism – and in the technological evolution which accompanied its practices – by the colossus Google, which has especially targeted the B2B (*business to business*) market with the offer of services to destinations and operators, mainly in marketing terms. Furthermore some services, like Google Maps, have certainly had a significant impact on tourism while attempted innovations, such as Google Glass, generated great expectations in this framework. The attention of the American multinational to tourism has always been high, therefore, as demonstrated by the countless studies of the sector produced by it and by its presence at the leading trade fairs and shows. Google's full entry into tourism was confirmed in 2016 with the launch of Destinations: the idea was to provide complete and immediate answers on the smartphone to all the questions which users usually ask when organising holidays (what the best time to depart is, price levels, weather, hotels, museums to visit, and so on). If done from a mobile, such searches become complicated as they mean opening lots of different windows and so also inhibit online booking processes. It is still not known what impact Google Destinations and other Google tourism products will have on the way tourism products are provided and sold. Google has got much more than just its eyes on the travel and holiday industry. According to some estimates it is already worth about $100 billion (Skift, 2017) for the colossus as it operates on several fronts, from simplification of meta-searches to online booking and simultaneous translation services.

What we have just sketched are about 170 years of the history of tourism.

Without going too far back in time, from the invention of low-cost flights that can be booked online, to Airbnb, there can be no dispute that the progresses in transport and the new economy have not only given a fundamental boost to the development of the sector, but have also radically transformed the business models.

A great deal of change has come about as a result of the geopolitical changes that have led to the opening of borders, from the Berlin Wall to Schengen, as well as the economic ones with the consolidation of travelling and holidays as a commodity. Combined with the rise in the levels of the average available income in many developing countries, this has produced millions of new tourists in many new markets.

From a traditional labour-intensive and capital-saving sector, today tourism has become the most advanced field of experimentation for the experience economy, for technological innovation applied to entertainment and the management of territories and flows, for the sharing economy and for architecture and engineering.

Notes

[1] Luciano Segreto, Carles Manera and Manfred Pohl, *Europe at the Seaside: The Economic History of Mass Tourism in the Mediterranean*, New York, Berghahn Books 2009, p. 174.

[2] B. Joseph Pine and James H. Gilmore, *The Experience Economy: Work is Theatre & Every Business a Stage*, Boston, Harvard Business Press, 1999, p. 70.

2   Tourism's New Geographies

What is often not seen in the classifications but which – of all the changes – is certainly one of the most fascinating to observe and most important to bear in mind for tourism competitiveness, is the phenomenon that has occurred in the last ten years in the physical geography of the new markets and new destinations.

To understand this it is sufficient to look at the UNWTO's forecasts for up to 2030 and the changes in the classification of the top international tourism spenders. In addition to the growth in world tourism starting from 1990, the former clearly reveal the centrality of Asia/Pacific in arrival terms, while the latter highlight the development of tourism from the BRIC countries (though India still remains secondary).

This geographical transformation has had two consequences: the enlargement of the market in terms of demand and the loss of share by the countries that have traditionally been receivers of tourism, to the benefit of new areas.

This change is obviously pregnant with implications for at least three reasons. Let's try to illustrate them by adopting, for simplicity, the outlook of a destination that is traditionally strong and consolidated on the tourism market, such as France or Italy.

The first implication is that many large new markets have opened in recent years, including China, South Korea, Brazil, Russia, Azerbaijan, the United Arab Emirates and many more. This is therefore great news for our hypothetical destination: if the cake is big, each slice will obviously seem larger. Even if it is necessary to take account of the fact that while some regions, such as South/ South-East Asia, are experiencing vibrant tourist development, much of the flow is nevertheless made up of trips within the area: e.g. Koreans going to China, or Chinese visiting Thailand.

Figure 1   Evolution of international arrivals in the world by geographical region

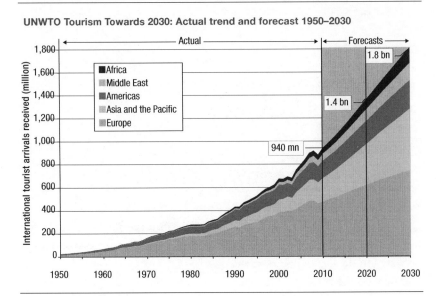

UNWTO Tourism Towards 2030: Actual trend and forecast 1950–2030

Source: UNWTO, 2018

Figure 2   World's top tourism spenders in 2017, billions USD

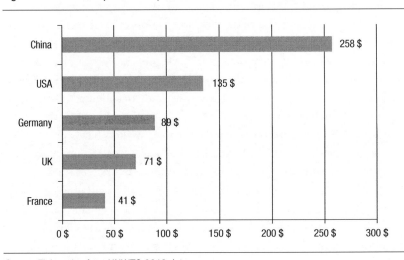

Source: Elaboration from UNWTO 2018 data

The second factor is that all these new markets are also new destinations. So, for example, if it is true that the growing Chinese middle class is travelling more and more, it is also true that China increasingly presents itself today as a leading tourism destination, placed fifth in the world for international arrivals.

This element is therefore a little less positive for our hypothetical destination: yes, the cake is bigger but there are now more people at the party. Are we sure that its slice still totally and exclusively belongs to it?

The third implication is not related to the size of the cake and of its slices, but the quality of the ingredients. In other words, the question we must ask is: what tourists do we want to attract and what are they looking for? How do they behave on the ground and what are we able to offer them? Do we know them well enough and are we competitive enough to give them what they seek? It is also a question of understanding the extent to which destinations are able to welcome them and are competitive as regards offering them what they expect.

Let's look at the case of a Korean tourist who decides to visit a European country such as Italy or France.

We have chosen the example of South Korea because it is a very interesting market for European destinations as a result of its powerful economic development and fast recovery from the 2008 crisis. Korean tourism in Europe is quite significant in absolute number and in constant growth in percentage terms. Koreans holidaying abroad, furthermore, are big spenders and are particularly attracted by "made in Europe" goods and typical local food and wine, a determinant factor for their tourism outlay.

Such tourists especially go online for inspiration and information. Not on Google in Korea, though, where it still plays a marginal role, but on Naver, the main search engine in South Korea with about 70% of market share. They will look for Venice, Rome, Paris or London on Naver and in the enormous Naver online communities. One of the widest read for tourism in Europe is Eurang, which offers information on transport, hotels or shopping in the continent's main destinations also on the basis of the type of trip: honeymoon, family, groups of friends, shopping, etc.

Naver and its cafés talk about Europe's romantic destinations like Italy, perfect for a honeymoon, rich in history and with monuments to admire. You eat well and it is a great destination for shopping. But they also tell us that in some countries public transport does not work very well, that bag snatchers are quite frequent in the main destinations, that food is dear and that it is difficult to book restaurants, that there is almost never information material in Korean and that the hotel rooms are often dirty and that the facilities do not work.

In order to make a booking once they had decided on their destination, until just a few years ago Korean tourists prevalently turned to agencies – such as Hana Tour, one of the biggest, or Hanjin – and purchased packages. Today, like their Western colleagues, they increasingly tended to organise their trips autonomously, after consulting Naver, and through the leading OTAs (online travel agencies) that focus on the Korean market: Expedia, for example, which launched in the country in 2013, recorded 80% growth in the first quarter of the following year. Mobile tourism booking is also growing rapidly.

However, Korean tourists still feel a little uncertain as regards the security of online booking in such distant countries. They therefore look for photographs, videos and clear information, and it is important for them to be able to chat and interact directly with the structures and operators, by messaging for example.

Getting to European destinations is not a problem: there are countless direct flights available and the range of connections to Europe is quite broad, while it is not necessary to obtain visas for most countries. This last point is critical and ensures ease of access and of transit in different European destinations: Chinese and Indian travellers, for example, have to apply for a visa before departure and the ease with which they can obtain one in one country rather than another strongly influences the choice of connection and therefore the lenght of stay in different locations.

If it is easier to obtain a visa for the Shengen area from the German embassy or consulate rather than from the Italian one, a tourist will opt to fly via Frankfurt rather than via Rome, with the associated knock-on effects in terms of stay and spend in the two countries. It should also be considered that in the case of very big countries like China, the diffusion of centres for visas across the land is also critical.

Then, on arrival at their chosen destination – Venice for example – what do tourists expect to find and what will they need?

First of all they are looking for Wi-Fi. They take it for granted and are accustomed to very high connection speeds: along with Hong Kong and Japan, South Korea is in fact among the world leaders for the diffusion of the Internet and the fastest connections with average speeds of 28.6 Mbps, i.e. 5.6 times faster than the world average.

Box 1   The role of the procedures for obtaining visas for the development
of international tourism

A country's access policies are among the factors that have the greatest influence on international tourism. The procedures and costs required for obtaining visas, and other travel documents such as passports, are in fact among the factors that affect the development of tourism.

Despite the fact that much progress has been made on the so-called facilitation front at international level in the last ten years, according to UNWTO about two-thirds of the world's population still need to obtain a visa before departure. Of the other third, one half can travel freely and the others need a visa on arrival in the destination country.

The types of tourist visa and the procedures for obtaining them vary considerably from country to country. In general, the rules that are toughest from the tourism stance are for Western countries as these are particularly sensitive to immigration and security questions, while the emerging economies tend to be more open in order to reinforce their competitiveness on the tourism market.

There has been a wide-ranging debate in the European Union since 2013 on revising visas in the Schengen area with a view to streamlining the issuing procedures in order to reinforce the links with other policies, such as those for tourism, and to further simplify the procedures for frequent travellers. Also being examined is the creation of a new type of visa, the "circulation visa", that would make it possible to stay in the territory of two or more Schengen States for more than 90 days but no more than one year (with the possibility of an extension for another year).

Moreover, the European Union is currently working on the "smart borders" programme for improving border controls and combatting irregular immigration, while at the same time facilitating border crossings for frequent travellers who have already been subject to preliminary security screening. To facilitate legitimate travelling without undermining security, the EU assigns sums to Member States as contributions to the internal border Security Fund. During the 2014–2020 period, a sum of €2.76 billion has been allocated to management of internal frontiers and the controls carried out at these borders, in order to combat irregular migration more effectively and guarantee better processing of Schengen visa applications.

However, the purpose of the visa application is not only linked to immigration policies and to guarantee security by controlling entries, their duration and motivations, but arises from political considerations regarding reciprocity between countries and also generates conspicuous returns. Finally, the visas issued constitute a means for controlling tourism demand and may be useful for supporting the definition of measures for guaranteeing the carrying capacity of the destination.

A good example of how a country's tourist competitiveness can be influenced by visa questions comes from Ireland where, thanks to an agreement with the United States, it is possible to complete all the customs formalities for entry into the USA directly at Dublin airport. This service, combined with the flight scheduling system of the flag carrier, Aer Lingus, that takes account of the connections between Dublin and US cities including New York, Boston, Chicago and Los Angeles, has reinforced the Irish capital's role as European gateway to the United States. Another example is provided by Finland and its strategy for positioning itself on the Chinese market: with its "StopOver Finland" programme, the country has aimed to become a stopover destination with the opening of 13 new visa centres in China while equipping itself to become a "cashless getaway" location, to make it as easy as possible for Chinese tourists to make payments at destination.

Wi-Fi is crucial for sharing their experience on social media but also for getting information on how to organise the trip: restaurants, museums, shopping and transport.

They then want to feel safe, and the need for security also extends to their bags, at least one of which will gradually fill with purchases made at destination. They are very demanding regarding the quality of the services, hospitality and information, and they can get particularly irritated – compared to more patient tourists – by delays and inefficiencies.

They also want to be recognised as Koreans and not confused with other Asian tourists and, while understanding English fairly well, they greatly appreciate getting at least basic information in their own language.

In the light of all this the question is therefore: do we know how to meet their needs? Are we able to tell them about our countries adequately? Can we surprise them and live up to their expectations? Do we know how to channel targeted proposals and communicate our offer adequately? These questions are not banal as it is only if all the answers are positive that a destination can consider itself to be truly competitive.

Of course the Korean tourist is only one example that highlights that as the geographies of tourism gradually change, the destinations are also required to measure themselves against new competitors if they are to attract visitors whose needs are increasingly diversified, who have holidays at different times of the year than we do, and therefore travel in different periods and have specific requirements, determined by their cultures of origin (a good example is the spa sector which has had to adapt its services to become Muslim-friendly).

As a consequence, many countries and many operators are taking action to improve their hospitality culture and innovate their services. This does not simply mean knowing how to greet and host tourists adequately,

Box 2   The development of the market in the East and digital marketing of tourism

Today, any assessment of the digital marketing of tourism must also include a reflection on the digital tools that are most appropriate for the various markets. If it is true in fact that there are over 4.1 billion Internet users and 3.8 unique mobile Internet users[1], only 2.1 of them use a Western platform like Facebook. What do the other 2 billion use?

The Chinese government's censorship of Google, YouTube, Facebook and Twitter has not really held back the digitisation of the market and it has simply developed other channels. China has almost 750 million Internet users and extremely high mobile phone use. The most widely used applications – hybrids of messaging and social media – are WeChat, Qzone and the Chinese version of Twitter called Sina Weibo. There are almost 570 million online video viewers: the social media for sharing videos is Youku Tudou, and attracts over 400 million visitors every month. Google is not available and in its place is Baidu.

In Russia too the digital panorama is very different to ours. Google is present, but it is mainly used as a foreign language search engine as the main search engine is Yandex. Russians prefer Vkontakte to Facebook and for booking hotels for their holidays they not only use Booking.com but also Ostrovok and OneTwoTrip.

but also to ensure that they have the right interpretative tools for enjoying a full and accessible experience, especially in destinations with strong cultural vocations: a visit to the Uffizi can be very different for a Dutch person than for an Indian!

It was from this awareness that the French took action, for example, with their *Do you speak touriste?* initiative which has become a case study: some surveys of tourist satisfaction with their stays, in fact, revealed that it was the Parisians themselves who were considered to be the real weak point in the tourist experience in France's capital. In 2013 the tourism authority of the Paris region therefore attempted to remedy the situation with a series of information brochures and a portal for operators in the sector, illustrating the needs of tourists from the various markets of reference, in order to improve the quality of hospitality in the city.

In 2015 this project was then followed by the creation of an app intended for the tourists themselves – Yes, I Speak Touriste – to help them to overcome linguistic and information barriers during their stay in Paris.

Are we ready for the globalisation of tourism (which is not the same thing as mass tourism)? This mutated geography of tourism brings the birth of new products and services along with it (as is the case for luxury

Figure 3   Do you speak Touriste?

cruises, wedding tourism, shopping tourism, etc.) and a strategic reflection: of the 1.2 billion international travellers, how many and which to we
want to welcome? Do we want the biggest slice of the cake or the best?
Do we want hordes of touch-and-go tourists, or do we want to attract
travellers motivated by a desire to discover new lands, with high spending
power, who purchase local products and who come back or stay longer?

Notes

[1] Source: Statista on We are Social, 2018.

3   DIY Tourists

Tourism, understood both as an industry and as a consumption habit, has therefore changed enormously in the last 20 years. The changes regard many aspects which we can trace very succinctly back to a variety of macro-contexts. As we have seen, one of these is geographical.

Then there is the development of ICT: this has impacted on every strand of the industry and triggered a process of radical transformation of the ways information is obtained by tourists, of the hospitality and promo-marketing processes and, more generally, of progressive disintermediation. Furthermore, today tourism is one of the leading sectors for e-commerce and for info-commerce: the online purchase of tourism packages, airline and rail tickets, holidays and all travel accessory services is in continuous expansion.

The other greatly evolving area concerns the characteristics of the demand: this has become increasingly exacting and more and more proficient, demanding and informed, interested in the experiential component of the trip and of the holiday, and in getting to know places. In fact tourists are looking for high-identity product destinations (or ones that appear so), unique and authentic experiences, even in mass destinations; they want to come into contact with the locals in order to experience their usages, and they are substantially omnivorous tourists who do not fall into the traditional boxes, i.e. cultural, seaside, mountains and so on.

This transformation of the tourist led, for example, to the development of many new forms of tourism, from so-called "creative tourism" – intended as a form of tourism linked to the fruition of contemporary culture – to slow tourism, from bicycle tourism to tours of production districts.

Then there is the progressive and intense affirmation of new and different forms of hospitality other than the hotel: these range from B&Bs and agritourism structures to Airbnb apartments, and from new hostels to de-signer hotels accompanied, finally, by the evolution of forms of transport.

These transformations are the most evident ones that have characterised tourism in recent times but every year other classifications are produced on the main trends in progress and on the major changes on the horizon.

The central role played by technology when purchasing and enjoying places, the desire for unique experiences, and hyper-customisation of the product, along with a return to simplicity, are often at the centre of these lists of travel trends. A transversal reading of the various classifications by macro-theme reveals that what influences the short-term future, at least on the demand side, is more or less as follows.

1.   Grey-haired globetrotters and generation Z

A first important datum regards the age of the tourists who travel around Europe and the world today, even if it is only recently that a real awareness has been developing of the importance of demographic changes and of their impact on the competitiveness of tourism systems.

Much has been said recently, for example, of the millennials – people born between the start of the 1980s and the early 2000s – and of how – with its expectations, lifestyles and confidence with technology – this generation is profoundly changing the ways of travelling and, as a conse-quence, what destinations offer.

However there are another two "generations" worthy of note, especially in perspective: seniors, i.e. citizens aged over 65,[1] and Generation Z, those born in from second half of the 1990s up to 2010.

Of the roughly 500 million citizens of the European Union today, about 20% are over 65 and 16% under 14. According to current forecasts, of 520 million Europeans in 2080, 29% will be aged over 65 and 15.2% under 14.

These figures should not necessarily be seen negatively ... Today's over-65s are the "most vigorous from the physical point of view and the most active in mental terms in the history of the Old World. Furthermore, from the technological and scientific viewpoint, it is unquestionably the best educated and most specialised generation of old people that Europe has ever had"[2] and, at least potentially, this fact constitutes an authentic eco-nomic launching pad for tourism too.

Half of European citizens aged over 65 travel at least once a year, in fact, and over time the number of tourists in this age bracket is increasing – as is the duration of their stays. They travel a lot inside their countries' borders, they love cultural trips and, if they can, they take holidays several times a year, preferably in low season.

The frequency and characteristics of the travels of these "grey-haired globetrotters" with purchasing power and leisure time, have led the European Union to maintain that their contribution to the tourism industry is indispensable for tackling, for example, the problem of seasonality, for stimulating economic growth and for promoting employment.[3]

Many countries such as Ireland, the UK and Germany, to mention just some European examples, or Australia and China, to look at other continents, have already equipped themselves to learn and better understand the habits of the over-65s – also in relation to factors such as level of education, ethnic background and state of health – and discover the main levers and services necessary for developing tourism for seniors, from improving the physical and cultural accessibility to places to the presence of adequate health structures in the destinations. The question of access to information technologies is particularly important for this target, for which the digital divide is still quite marked but will probably be overcome in the course of a few years.

The generational question in the tourism world goes well beyond seniors. The other phenomenon, in fact, is linked to the development of tourism for the post-millennials, namely those born from the second half of the 1990s up to 2010. Since 2016, many of them still have not had a job or are not even at university but, by 2020, will have $44 billion in their pockets, the result of weekly pocket money and the income from occasional jobs.[4] They make up one-sixth of the world's population and, in developed countries, already travel on their own or, if younger, have a critical influence on their family's travel decisions.

As regards the new tourism of children and teenagers, this is affected not so much by demographic trends – unfavourable in this case – but by the profound changes in lifestyles and the greater accessibility of many destinations. These in turn are the result of changes in transportation and a more open and knowledgeable mentality of families which are more willing than before to permit – or indeed encourage – their children's desire for travel with the conviction that, even generically, this constitutes an educational plus.

The few available figures on these young tourists shows that demand is increasing and the age when they start travelling is getting lower: now it is a normal phenomenon for children to travel alone, also as a result of professionalisation of families vis-à-vis travelling as those who are used to travelling look on the experience of children as being normal on their own going away. At the age of eight they already travel abroad on study trips and the minimum threshold for going away with friends – according to statistics – has dropped to 14; in the meantime the younger ones (post Generation Z) are content to agree with their parents on the destination and means of travel, before they too can leave home carrying their own bags.

The fact that parents can guarantee themselves a few breaks from strict supervision/care/guidance of their children during the course of the holiday, channels them towards destinations that offer specific tailor-made activities for them. This does not necessarily mean purely recreational activities such as today's ubiquitous baby clubs or playrooms, nor ad hoc destinations such as the amusement parks which have also experienced a boom in recent years, but also activities that are constructively specific in the cultural sense.

While waiting for the youngest to grow up, operators and destinations are keeping their eye on Generation Z as its needs will certainly presage

Figure 1   Influence of kids on family travel plans, selected countries

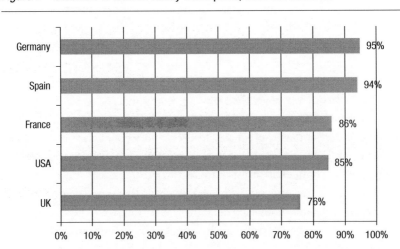

Source: Elaboration from HomeAway 2015 data

great changes both because of the desire to distinguish itself from previous generations and because of its characterising features: Generation Z love messaging more than any other social media (better if incognito using applications like Snapchat and Whisper), they prefer Instagram to Facebook and Twitter and, above all, their brain processes information more quickly than their older siblings and parents ... even if they retain the information less.[5] The marketing of tourism must adapt itself first.

2. DIY tourists v organised tourists

IT has been a disruptive factor in terms of the ways people get information and purchase tourist services. On the supply side this has led to online direct and intermediating booking processes, with the affirmation of online travel agency (OTA) services and, on the demand side, to the constantly greater autonomy of tourists when choosing and organising their holidays, especially for short and medium-range trips.

This freedom and activism when putting trips together has then been further accentuated by the ubiquity of mobile phones and diffusion of mobile booking.

Today's tourists book from home but also when they are at their destination, they book while at work, from the tube train and in bed before going to sleep. Amid all this digital hyperactivity, focussed on fine-tuning the travel experience, we have progressively also seen the abandonment of a monolithic conception and typological pigeonholing of the holiday with multiplication of approaches to tourism. This is because tourists have actually become more unfaithful to themselves, shifting part of their focus from "where" to go towards "what" to do: if they are at the seaside this does not mean that they consider themselves to be seaside holiday-makers and, even here, they still want to visit art exhibitions, take food and wine tours or climb indoor climbing walls, as well, obviously, as sunbathe on the beach. As a result, aspects that are generally considered not very "touristy" take on greater importance for tourists looking for original experiences and sensations, and new "uncategorised" tourism proposals are created: from charm hostels to glamping, a word that blends "glamorous" and "camping" and indicates new super-luxury camping sites to Shinrin-yoku – a Japanese term that can be translated as "forest bathing" – and to farm tourism.

This self-organised tourism is characterised by a profound transformation of people's mental processes and decision-making mechanisms with the affirmation of "professional" attitudes to holidays attitudes such as, for example, the assiduous recourse to apps dedicated to weather forecasts (a practice that also has impacts on hotel revenue management!).

However, the arrival of DIY tourism has not meant the disappearance of the organised sector and this still constitutes an important share of flows, especially the long-haul ones. Furthermore, new luxury organised tourism has been asserting itself with the development of South-East Asian tourism.

3.   Attention to sustainability

As with other sectors of the economy, demand has also grown considerably in the tourism sector for eco-compatible products and services starting from the 1990s: more and more tourists want to be informed about the environmental characteristics of the locations they visit; they are interested in the environmental (and social) performance of the hospitality structures they stay in and want their holiday to have the lowest possible impact on local ecosystems. For the moment, this phenomenon has mainly been recorded in industrialised countries but it is also spreading today in many developing countries.

Tourists are becoming more aware of their environmental footprint and select and appreciate green solutions – *alberghi diffusi*, agritourism, camping sites, eco hotels – and forms of tourism that are able to offer an authentic experience that respects the destinations.

It is in this context that we should read the great international success of slow tourism: according to the UNWTO slow tourism involves people travelling to destinations more slowly, staying longer and travelling less; they complete their trip within the borders of their destination as an experience in itself, and when they have arrived they use local transport, enjoy "slow food and drink" and dedicate time to learning the history and culture of the locality (UNWTO).

The supply side is adjusting as a consequence, motivated on the one hand by the acquisition of an awareness of the effects of potentially compromising the environment as a key resource for tourism but, on the other, especially by strictly competitive pressures that regard the need to differentiate the service. In a sector with an enormous number of competitors with similar characteristics, the quality of the environment is in fact seen as an opportunity for differentiating the service and exploring new market niches.

4.   Food and Wine as a central element in the travel experience

Also partially linked to the theme of the environment is the subject of food (and wine) that has pervaded tourism since the middle of the 2000s.

Figure 2   Food experience destination portals, Slovenia and Denmark

Denmark: A Nordic Foodie Paradise

Punching well above its weight for a country of under six million inhabitants, Denmark is a culinary destination known world-wide. The country is home to the New Nordic movement, which prizes seasonality and respect for local, high-quality ingredients, so it's no surprise Denmark boasts 31 Michelin Stars and 26 star-studded restaurants to choose from. And thankfully, this philosophy extends to the vibrant street food scene where you can try foods of all sorts without breaking the bank. Denmark is truly a foodie's paradise.

To appreciate this it is enough to enter any tourism office and leaf through the brochures or look at any of the travel magazines on sale or distributed on trains and planes. On the other hand, in an increasingly digital world, food – with its smells, flavours, colours and consistencies – and the "industry of taste" are able, more than any other products and services, to generate differentials in which consumption is increasingly linked to the cultural elements of a place or to the sensorial experience.

As a result, food and wine tourism has achieved enormous success and a geographic and typological expansion in the last 15 years, with the creation of a great variety of proposals and a constant evolution of the types of offer. Simply think of the experience of various Italian regions like Tuscany or Piedmont, or countries such as Spain, France and Ireland: it is no longer a case of wine roads and or events linked to taste but of complex offer systems that integrate opportunities linked to the food and wine culture, to the creative industries, to culture and to active experiences with the participation of tourists themselves.

There are countless examples of proposals that have sprung up around food. They range from museums of taste, to "creative events" linked to food, to architectural tours of wineries, to street food and the products that involve the tourist's direct participation: courses of regional cooking in catering venues and private houses, or experiential family-friendly proposals in farm locations; some of these experiences have also sprung up and are developing thanks to the new technological supports and platforms of the sharing economy.

Box 1   The new experiential wine tourism

Wine tourism is one of the great areas in expansion today and is particularly interesting as it provides a laboratory for trying out new forms of receptivity and hospitality, and of products in general, that encapsulate some of the key aspects of new tourism trends: wellbeing, luxury, design, culture, nature and food.

"Wine & food tourism perhaps constitutes one of the most hedonistic aspects of tourism, given that wine consumption tout court only constitutes the last step in a sensorial trip that embraces the landscape, company hospitality, visit to the winery and tasting."*

In recent years the benefits deriving from wine tourism are flowing well beyond the winery doors to benefit the entire local economy, creating employment in tourism, favouring the development of local unions, stimulating innovation in tourism supply and the other complementary forms of tourism, such as food tourism, slow tourism and, above all, cultural tourism, contributing in a sometimes crucial manner to place-branding strategies in a process for the transformation of "landscapes" into "brandscapes".

This is particularly evident in those territories that are capable of capitalising on the proactivity of the food and wine businesses and introducing experiential and cultural elements unto the private and public offering. In this way, they exploit, to their own benefit, the need increasingly felt by the wineries to create a bond with customers not simply on the basis of the product but also of the drinking experience. This can be done, for example, by designing itineraries for the discovery of the production process, the architecture and design of the wineries and the exploitation of the wine landscape with the organisation of cultural events in the establishments themselves and offering packages that combine hospitality, spas and wellness.

There are many examples at international level from the Napa Valley with the architecture of Herzog and de Meuron and the wine design resorts, to the Rioja region, where the structures and furnishings of the wineries bear the signatures of world-famous architects and designers like Santiago Calatrava, Zaha Hadid or Norman Foster, or the Tuscan wineries by Mario Botta and Renzo Piano. Not to mention museums, exhibition areas and visitor centres dedicated to wine such as La Cité du Vin in Bordeaux, the WiMU museum in Barolo, the Vivanco Museum of Wine Culture and many others.

Figure 3   Toscana Wine Architecture destination portal

* Boatto V., Gennari A.J. (2011), *La roadmap del turismo enologico*, Franco Angeli, Milan, p. 9.

Notes

[1] Some definitions lower the entry threshold to 55 however.
[2] Eberstadt e Groth, 2007.
[3] http://ec.europa.eu/enterprise/sectors/tourism/tourism-seniors/index_it.htm
[4] www.skyft.com
[5] Skift, Megatrends 2016.

4 Technology and Playful Learning to Enjoy Locations and their Attractions

Technology is obviously a key factor as regards these trends in the demand, but it cannot be read only as an enabling tool for DIY tourism: it has much more pervasive effects on the structure of the sector, on the construction of tourism products and services, on the promotion and sale of destinations, on the management of flows and, in general, on destination management, with the employment of liquid and porous processes that channel demand and supply into continuous interaction and collaboration.

On one hand the interaction between tourism and ICT manifests itself in innovative forms of advertising and promotion/marketing of places and tourism services. On the other, infrastructuring is created in a rich and diversified manner to aid enjoyment of the destinations and for imagining new ways of channelling tourist contents and services.

During the pre-experience stage, the tourist-consumer is influenced by the institutional and other information available online.

During the trips, technology intervenes both to support the experience – this is the case, for example, of advanced signage, gaming, mobility apps, maps, augmented reality, interactive museums and immersive environments but also digital wallets for mobile payment – and for sharing the experience itself on social media or reviewing apps, etc.

And then, finally, comes the return home from the trip or holiday. And so technology also plays a role in the post-experience: for uploading videos and photos, for putting together travel blogs and for leaving online comments and reviews.

To better understand how all this translates in concrete terms and to exemplify it, let us attempt to identify the stages that each of us goes through when we are transformed into tourists. We could list at least five:

Figure 1   The five stages of the travel cycle and associated activities

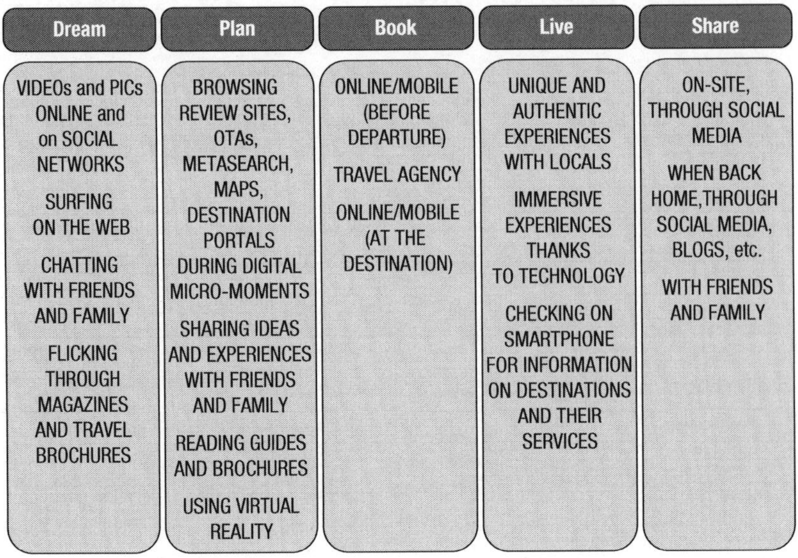

Dream	Plan	Book	Live	Share
VIDEOs and PICs ONLINE and on SOCIAL NETWORKS SURFING ON THE WEB CHATTING WITH FRIENDS AND FAMILY FLICKING THROUGH MAGAZINES AND TRAVEL BROCHURES	BROWSING REVIEW SITES, OTAs, METASEARCH, MAPS, DESTINATION PORTALS DURING DIGITAL MICRO-MOMENTS SHARING IDEAS AND EXPERIENCES WITH FRIENDS AND FAMILY READING GUIDES AND BROCHURES USING VIRTUAL REALITY	ONLINE/MOBILE (BEFORE DEPARTURE) TRAVEL AGENCY ONLINE/MOBILE (AT THE DESTINATION)	UNIQUE AND AUTHENTIC EXPERIENCES WITH LOCALS IMMERSIVE EXPERIENCES THANKS TO TECHNOLOGY CHECKING ON SMARTPHONE FOR INFORMATION ON DESTINATIONS AND THEIR SERVICES	ON-SITE, THROUGH SOCIAL MEDIA WHEN BACK HOME, THROUGH SOCIAL MEDIA, BLOGS, etc. WITH FRIENDS AND FAMILY

dreaming, planning, booking, the experience itself, the return and sharing everything about it all with those who weren't with us physically.

In each of these stages – dreaming of a trip and possible destinations, planning and booking, sharing what we are experiencing with others – it is possible to see how the technological aspects have become fundamental for constructing our experience as travellers.

1.   Dreaming and planning

How do we approach the idea of going away and how to we come to choose a destination? In the past we used to talk to friends or relations about their travel experiences or their favourite places, or we went to a travel agency and came back home with tons of catalogues to flick through on the couch, with their pictures of crystalline seas, golden beaches and exotic landscapes.

Things have changed quite a lot today, but really not so much in some ways: the main difference is that word or mouth, which has always been the first source when choosing trips and holidays, has gone from local to global and from real to virtual, in other words: people look for inspiration in their friends' and colleagues' posts on Facebook and Instagram, in blogs and online communities, etc.

Unlike the past, however, it is not just the photographs that fire people's travel fantasies, but also and above all video clips: more and more often these are conditioning decisions about where to go and what to do once there. The operators and destinations have adapted themselves as a result, using teaser videos, web series and films to promote themselves.

For a few years now the Internet has become the primary source of inspiration for deciding where to go on holiday and not just for comparative purposes – for example when I decide on a trip to Greece and then navigate to find somewhere specific to go to – but for absolute ones, i.e. people begin searching online before deciding where or how to travel.

Finally, it is interesting to note how the use of social media to seek travel inspiration and useful information for planning holidays has also contributed to establishing it as a tool for organising group holidays, especially for people who are geographically remote but connected online.

It is not just social media that is used when organising breaks along with friends in our online communities, but also dedicated new tools such as Travefy or Tripit, or other apps designed for organising trips for bigger groups on occasions such as weddings, for example.

Another great difference from even the recent past is that while searches are made online it is increasingly common, however, for us to do so via smartphone during our digital "micro-moments", i.e. the time windows during which people almost instinctively turn to a device – more and more often the smartphone – to meet a need: learn how to do something, obtain information, buy something. The moments, that Google calls "moments that count", are particularly important precisely because of their motivational content and are therefore strategic from a marketing stance, for reaching consumers with proposals, offers and responses that are adequate and, especially, immediate and not time-consuming. Whether it is the PC or the smartphone, only a part of search for information is limited to a single screen: the simultaneous use of the PC, tablet and phone, and even the TV is an established and growing phenomenon ("multi-screening"). It is utilised for a whole series of activities that range from consulting maps to reaching places of interest, to reading online hotel and restaurant reviews and to checking in online.

2. Booking

Like seeking information, booking is also (and especially) primarily done online nowadays, almost always in the case of short-range self-organised trips. And it is increasingly done using travel apps that have been growing exponentially since 2015.

According to a Google survey,[1] in 2017 over 40% of smartphone users in the USA, UK and France felt at ease seeking, booking and planning their entire trip to a new destination using a mobile device only. These percentages rose to over 50% in countries like South Korea and Japan and to almost 70% in countries like Brazil.

In this picture the lion's share is taken by OTAs which have very significant shares in every region of the world: meta-search apps such as Expedia, Booking.com, Skyscanner or Kayak, and Trainline have a significantly higher number of direct distributors like airlines, for example. However it is very possible that there will be a resurgence of direct booking, especially for services/stays that require much more complexity/customisation than a simple bed-night. In direct booking's favour is also the direct contact it provides with the structures/companies offering the service. Tourists increasingly desire such contact, as shown by the success of instant messaging in tourism and that of those travel companies that have added features to their apps in order to enhance the travel experience and reconnect with their most loyal customers.

Instant messaging and apps provide an important opportunity for the cultivation of direct relationships with customers by extending contact throughout the customer journey.

Instant messaging has been the fastest-growing social behaviour in recent years and, above all, since 2013, with higher growth rates than social networks, as demonstrated by the evolution in the use of such tools as WhatsApp, WeChat, Snapchat and others, compared to Instagram for example.

The opportunities these tools offer tourism operators are clearly enormous as they make it possible to enter into direct and personal contact with customers, especially in order to provide on-demand, tailor-made services and support and to increase direct bookings.

Chinese tourists, for example, are accustomed to using WeChat for checking in at hotels, and for booking trains and other means of transport. At the beginning of 2016, Dan Moriarty, a social media strategist in the Hyatt hotel group, told the Skift online magazine that they had received 50,000 WeChat messages from customers in 2015. Of these, 60% were questions linked to their stay and about 40% were about the booking.

The use of instant messaging for purchases and for marketing information is still not so widespread in the West, but there can be no doubt that it soon will be. It is above all a question of creating a habit, and if messaging applications are already an integral part of our day, at work or leisure, their use for solving the practical and commercial aspects of our holidays is just around the corner too.

We are already prepared mentally: in reality the logic is the same as that underlying requests for information to smart assistants like Siri and Google Assistant or the messages from taxi or Uber drivers that notify us of their arrival, or from Amazon Prime that inform us about delivery times. In the near future it will seem natural and indispensable for us to ask our hotel if they have remembered to put a baby cot in the room, to check that our bags have been transferred from one plane to another during an airport stopover or, simply to book a room.

Figure 2 Most popular mobile messaging apps worldwide, based on number of monthly active users (in millions)

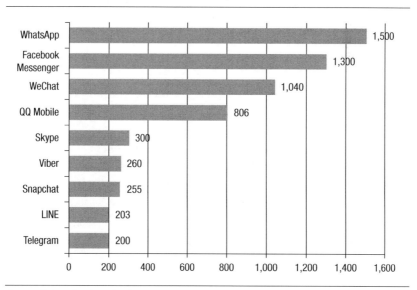

Source: Elaboration from Statista, July 2018 data

3.   Living

Technology has also profoundly changed our way of living our holiday and of getting around the locality of our destination. This is above all because of the travel apps mentioned above, which are expanding with vastly different offers in terms of both content and format.

On the format front, for example, we may have apps that provide information through augmented reality, videos or sound clips. In content terms, on the other hand, there are apps that are mainly designed for planning the holiday or for providing information on the destination, on its historical and artistic heritage, or on the events, or others to experience them through games. Some applications also create direct links between the destination attractors and more commercial aspects linked to entertainment or regional products. Finally, new apps today, also linked to the sharing economy world, are able to put tourists in contact with one another or with residents in order to share services or experiences.

Central to this once again is the smartphone.

The computing and memory capacities of smartphones and the power of their various constituent technological elements have made them into tools with enormous potential in the tourism field and for the exploitation of information that reaches users automatically at the moment in which certain situations arise. Using specific programs via their smartphone, the app can interact with the external environment and from it, or rather through it, receive information and clarifications and itself become an element that interacts with the information provided by the outside world.

All this springs from the intrinsic features of smartphones, in particular:

- the ability to connect to the internet WiFi and therefore to huge databases that let the devices learn that certain conditions and certain information exists in that specific position;
- from incorporated hi-res photographic systems;
- from the ability to obtain the geographical coordinates (also with high precision from the GPS and/or Galileo satellite system) of their location (georeferencing);
- from fairly big screens to which commands can be transmitted by touch and gesture.

Thanks to these features it is possible, for example, to create augmented reality systems with interesting applications in the tourism sector, ranging from information/promotion, to entertainment, booking and socialisation with other users/tourists nearby.

Augmented reality essentially consists of the possibility of taking what the camera views or the map of your location and superimposing images, objects, information and things to do (interactions) that are retrieved from the databases and that are linked to your position. The app user can then learn if there are others in the vicinity who are using it and then interact with them and with the surrounding environment. Augmented reality has a multiplicity of uses in tourism: it can be used by tourists to obtain information on the services around them, such as bars, hotels or restaurants; it can constitute a useful support when visiting cultural sites and museums for obtaining details of what you are looking at, or can enrich the playfulness of the tourism experience using gaming applications applied to tourism contexts.

However mobile apps do not constitute the only informative and entertainment tool for exploring a destination but increasingly constitute a tool for facilitating and completing commercial transactions linked to shopping and sales of tickets for attractions, museums and public transport. They are therefore tools for simplifying the tourism experience that are particularly important for tourism counterparties who use different currencies and who are already established users of electronic payment systems.

It is no coincidence that many European destinations that are interested in attracting greater shares of Chinese tourists have taken action to ensure widespread implementation of systems such as Alipay – China's biggest mobile payment platform – or WeChat Pay. This is the case in Finland which, along with Finnair too, has promoted the implementation of countless attractions and commercial businesses also with local taxi companies.

Alipay, in particular, can be found in about 20 European countries and its tax-refund system is available at over 70 European airports.

4. Sharing

Finally, technology is a tool for sharing the experience – through blogs, online reviews, videos, comments and, above all, images posted on social media, etc. – both from the destination and after returning home. All these experiences are evidently interwoven and interact with the local supply and marketing worlds which promote, enhance and construct their products using technology.

Table 1 recaps the main technological aspects involved in the promotion, marketing and construction of tourist destinations and experiences.

Among the great many new and not so new technologies applied to promotion and to tourist information, a brief mention should be made of virtual reality which is also enjoying a period of growing success in tourism. Virtual reality – intended as a set-up that simulates a real situation which the user feels part of and with which they can interact by means of extremely sophisticated interfaces such as goggles or masks – offers original opportunities to tourism operators for entertaining their clients with the creation of new experiences: these may be complementary to real ones, for testing products and increasing sales and for facilitating and enriching the purchasing process with generated experiences.

Interesting examples of these two modes of utilisation of virtual reality come, for example, from Amadeus which announced in 2017 that it was at work on the world's first virtual reality travel search and booking experience, or from Lufthansa, but there are also interesting experiments going on in the destination world, as in the case of the tourism bodies of South Africa and Wales among others.

One of the limits to full development of virtual reality at the moment springs from the costs and quality of images, but costs are dropping rapidly, both on the devices front – just think of the cost of an Oculus headset – and on that of the development of the necessary applications. It is therefore expected that examples of implementation of virtual reality in tourism and for the enjoyment of destinations and cultural attractors will multiply in the coming years, even if development has been much slower than expected for the moment.

On the offer side, the technology is not only suitable for promotion and marketing, but also for controlling the territory and managing flows.

Technological tools are in fact used for monitoring and guiding tourists, for identifying and studying tourists and for studying the areas of congestion and providing mobility services, for example by means of big data analyses or with the development of artificial intelligence and the Internet of Things (IoT) which, along with and in coordination with wearable devices, promise to be sensational in the coming years.

Table 1   Technological aspects of the promotion and marketing of tourism destinations and attractors

Promotion/ information	Institutional sites of destinations/DMO sites Operators' institutional sites Blogs Social media Apps Virtial reality (VR) Mobile-TV; web-TV; social media-TV
Marketing	Institutional sites of destinations/DMO sites Operators' institutional sites Online tour operators/online travel agencies Mobile booking Mobile payment
Experience creation / interaction with the tourist	Institutional sites of destinations/destination marketing organisations sites Online thematic channels/via cable and satellite Smart signage Apps (mobility, augmented reality, destination apps, guides, gaming, experiences, booking) Virtual reality (VR) Instant messaging Virtual reality AI
Management	Georeferencing of flows Big data analyses Social communities/ mobile crowdfunding Urban sensing AI
Reputation	Online destination reputation monitoring Online reputation monitoring of structures and operators

The Internet of Things will let increasingly smart destinations provide travellers with relevant experiences and information in real time, thereby allowing them to make better use of their time, and will constitute a tool for more efficient and sustainable management of tourist flows, for example by providing specific services only when needed.

Moreover, technology can be a medium for collecting funds for the maintenance and management of tourism attractors through crowdfunding operations.

The subject of technology is therefore a key aspect of tourism development today, but it is also the case for the world of culture as the digital revolution is taking root, changing consumption behaviours, obliging many institutions from museums to theatres and festivals, to reconsider their relationship with the public and the models for spreading and enjoying the cultural contents of their products.

Technology is used in a more strictly cultural framework for building spaces for interactive and virtual experiences, for enjoying live experiences of things that no longer exist; for providing greater access to cultural assets that can no longer be experienced live and for offering cultural content and information on site and remotely. Finally, ICT provides an enormous opportunity for cultural heritage in terms of the development of governance and funding tools.

Note

[1]   https://www.thinkwithgoogle.com/consumer-insights/consumer-travel-smart-phone-usage/.

5   From Sharing Tourists to Sharing Economy

Increasingly demanding tourists with newer and newer needs, seeking unusual experiences, are creating new challenges for operators in the sector.

On the one hand, in fact, it is becoming more and more difficult to manage the reputational and communicative effects of the online activities of tourists who publish their travel experiences: they post impressions, they review hotels, restaurants and destinations, scathingly or enthusiastically, and they create new paths and new maps with their social profiles. On the other hand it is necessary to renew the offer in order to remain abreast with the requests and expectations of the travellers (increasingly numerous) that do not concern only and necessarily the more specifically and traditionally touristic experiences, but also everything else around them. This might include, for example, the simplicity of collecting information and clear indications, the ease of access to localities and regions, the availability of certain supplementary services and, increasingly, the opportunities for interacting with locals.

One of the most interesting phenomena in this context in recent years has been the development of the tourism sharing economy. This has in fact found considerable space in tourism for growth and for testing new models and activities.

This is no coincidence. Let's imagine an interesting destination but one that is touristically complicated because its mobility services are inefficient and do not permit tourists to move around easily and visit points of interest. Then, one day an urban car-sharing service is established or a road transport service that can be booked by app becomes available: everything changes.

Or, imagine the case of a small attractive provincial town with a rich historical-artistic heritage and excellent venue for an important arts festival. The hospitality on offer is normally more than sufficient but on the days of the event it becomes impossible to find a free room. Some residents decide to grasp the opportunity and make rooms in their homes available to tourists via an online platform. Once again everything changes.

The new technologies and business models underlying the sharing economy have given rise to a great transformation of tourism by offering people original accommodation, mobility and visiting options with the creation of economic opportunities for new people.

1.   The complex world of the sharing economy

The term "sharing" nevertheless leaves ample space for a whole range of different interpretations: the sharing economy umbrella actually covers phenomena that may be linked from case to case to collaborative consumption, on-demand services, to the rental economy and to the peer-to-peer economy.

The sharing economy umbrella covers thousands of highly differing operators and organisations, a galaxy of cooperatives, non-profit organisations, and small, medium and big businesses that have sprung up and developed especially in North America and Europe, but also in Asia, the Middle East and South America.

In just a few years some of these have become clearly profit-oriented giants that operate and prosper all over the world.

The figures for this part of the sharing economy are truly impressive: the revenues generated in Europe in 2015 in the five principal sectors – collaborative financing, accommodation in private houses, private transport, domestic services on request and professional services on request – amounted to €28 billion.[1] What is most impressive however is the dynamic of their growth. Transactions linked to the sharing economy will be worth €570 billion by 2025. We are witnessing a truly global phenomenon that is deeply rooted in society and therefore structural, with extraordinary prospects for growth.

Other structures were also created and grown, though with more modest dimensions and dynamics in various field and with authentic sharing, social utility and sustainability values. In the latter case, they may be private or public organisations with a clear non-profit vocation.

This second group is growing, though at a more relaxed pace. Most cases regard platforms that make it possible to share information and services;

they almost always have a non-profit ethos and are attentive to the values of the land, of sustainability and the common good. This second platform type operates in sectors relating to physical accessibility and urban connectivity, citizen information, the cultural offer, development of networks and the collection of funds for social goals.

A good example of this type is bike sharing which has spread today to all the main cities in Europe and around the world. This not only offers an economical service that is appreciated by townspeople but also contributes towards reducing traffic and pollution in town centres and stimulates communities towards more sustainable behaviours.

Taken together, all the sharing economy organisations oversee very different frameworks and sectors: from mobility to services for the community, from catering to hospitality, from fund-raising to the use of leisure time. It is nevertheless possible to identify common features. First of all they offer services without intermediaries. Secondly, these platforms employ reputational and quality control criteria that are specific to social networks: consumers express their views and appraisals of the services offered in such a way as to guide future users and, as a consequence, guarantee that the quality of the service is high and constantly monitored. Finally, the element that virtually all the operators in the sharing economy have in common is that they have managed, thanks to the new platforms available, to activate and market goods and services that would otherwise have been excluded from the economic circuit.

The new technologies and the new business and consumption models underlying the sharing economy are giving rise to a great transformation in tourism by offering people original accommodation, mobility and visiting options. They create business opportunities for new parties that connect with and amplify the recent trend to develop tourism experiences off the beaten path as it were, i.e. away from the consolidated destinations, while making use, moreover, of unconventional services.

2.   The sharing economy and tourism

The picture of the tourism sharing economy is multi-faceted with the participation of a variety of structures. On the one hand there are the profit-oriented private organisations such as Airbnb that operate in the hospitality sector, or BlaBlaCar, in transport. On the other is a world of operators with a profile that cannot always be linked to figures and frameworks in the tourism sector and closer to the economic sphere of gifts and bartering.

If, then, the tourism sharing economy has developed above all thanks to the role played by technological innovation, an extremely important driver for the growth of the sector has been the evolution in recent years in tourism demand, in other words in the ways and mindsets with which travellers face and live the journey and the holiday: in particular their growing attention to contemporary cultural output, to creative experiences and, in particular, to ways of discovering places where they can play a more active role in the composition and creation of the tourism experience. In parallel, the success of lots of new tools offered by the platforms of the sharing economy has also had a significant input into tourism and the behaviours of tourists. Over time, as the expectations for the quality and variety of services offered grew on the supply side, a huge number of new structures sprang up with greater and greater diversification of the products, services and prices on the supply side. This dynamic contributed in parallel with the development of various lesser-known destinations, outside traditional tourism circuits which, thanks to the sharing platforms, achieved both visibility and the answer to infrastructural shortcomings (for example, lack of beds or transport services). Moreover, studies of the sector such as those carried out by the OECD indicate that even in the more consolidated destinations the sharing economy is giving rise to longer stays, to a drop in seasonality, and to greater economic and employment development, also without large investments, and to new business opportunities for parties outside the sector.

The scenario is therefore a very interesting one for a heterogeneous series of actors, from market operators to exponents of the cultural association world, and from residents to tourists (both intended in the broad sense), even if there is no shortage of problems linked in particular to the new competitive picture which has been created and to governing it from regulatory and taxation standpoints. Furthermore, some studies are beginning to reveal the possible negative effects of the link between the sharing economy and tourism that extend over various urban dynamics: some platforms, in fact, would seem to accelerate and amplify residential segregation processes.

Also particularly interesting are the implications of the sharing economy for destinations in terms of coordination of new stakeholders who do

Box Airbnb and the invention of feeling at home anywhere

A conference of the Industrial Design Society of America was held in San Francisco in 2007. The hotels in the vicinity of the event were all full. Brian Chesky and Joe Gebbia, who attended the Rhode Island School of Design together, decided to rent out a room in their house for the occasion and pocket a little money towards paying the rent. These were the first steps of Airbnb as it was from this idea that the pair, along with their friend, Nathan Blecharczyk, founded the Airbedandbreakfast.com portal which later became Airbnb.com (2008). Today Airbnb is the symbol of the sharing economy for tourism, also because of the impact its entry into the market has had in terms of debates and reflections on the regulation and taxation policies. It is a symbol that has spread to 81,000 cities, in over 190 countries, and with 2 million people staying on Airbnb per night. In May 2015 the Obama administration appointed Chesky as Presidential Ambassador for Global Entrepreneurship.

Airbnb's range of action has diversified rapidly: from houses, to experiences and to the organisation of trips, still inspired by the philosophy of feeling at home anywhere, for leisure tourists but also for business ones, confirming that the search for authentic experiences will be at the core of "tourisms", at least for a while.

not belong directly to the tourism sector, but who have rapidly become key interlocutors for the tourism development of areas. This is the case of the so-called locals (from those who make their homes available on Airbnb, to those who offer themselves as professional guides for taking tourists to experience destinations in an authentic manner). In this way, tourism, especially in the experiential sense, stimulates an original shift away from the cultural assets (perceived as the significant element) to the person involved (the person who guarantees the experience).

If, on the one hand, the sharing economy developed above all thanks to the role of technological innovation and of other tools offered by the platforms, another extremely important driver of growth in the sector was found to be the evolution in recent years of tourist demand, i.e. of the ways and mentalities with which travellers tackle and experience their journeys and holidays today, with a new cultural and experiential approach. In this way tourism has become a natural testbed for the whole world of services for mobility and transport, accommodation and hospitality, catering and travel experiences. At the same time, the success of lots of new tools offered by the sharing economy platform has also had a significant input into tourism and the behaviour of tourists in a self-nourishing circle. As the expectations for the quality and variety of services offered grew, a huge number of new structures sprang up on the supply side with greater and greater diversification of the products, services and prices.

This dynamic not only stimulated the services world but contributed concomitantly to the development of various less famous, more affordable destinations, outside traditional tourism circuits which, thanks to the sharing economy, achieved both visibility and the answer to infrastructural shortcomings (for example, lack of beds or transport services). The scenario is therefore a very interesting one for market operators and for tourists alike.

Even if these changes are taking place extremely quickly, the incidence of the sharing economy on tourism in percentage terms is still marginal compared to the enormous turnover generated by the entire sector, but in the course of the next five to ten years the sharing economy will have a crucial effect on tourism. Over 500 platforms in the tourism sector already operate on the market: half of these are involved in transport, 40% in leisure services and 10% in hospitality. All this raises important questions for policymakers who already recognise the need for a better definition of the regulatory framework within which the sharing economy can and must operate ... starting from a more precise identification and definition of the sector, and of the categories of operators in it and of their different goals and strategies.

Another fundamental matter that has still not been faced adequately and which must be tackled soon concerns how the figures for the sharing economy are obtained. At the moment these are provided almost exclusively by the platforms themselves and despite from generic declarations of willingness they are still not very transparent. Therefore there are no wide-ranging and detailed studies of the sector or development forecasts provided by impartial third-party study centres.

The topic that emerges overwhelmingly more than any other is unquestionably that of rules and regulations.

Traditional operators working in tourism do so in many countries that have highly complex regulatory frameworks, the result of years of continuous adaptations to a frequently burdensome legislative scenarios: commercial licences, quality standards and controls, hygiene, health, safety, protection and guarantees for workers, taxation, insurance cover, environmental sustainability and much else. Rules that, for now, have not been applied to the new sharing platforms, arousing the justified protests of hoteliers, taxi drivers and all the so-called traditional operators, who complain of the absence of a fair competitive framework.

Table 1   Some figures from the tourism sharing economy

	Platform	Number of users	Annual turnover	Geographical area of operation
Hospitality	**Airbnb**	5 million listings worldwide 400 million guest arrivals all-tine (2018)	The total revenues amounted to 250 million dollars in 2013	Global: 191 countries
	HomeAway	1.5 million vacation rental listings	906.5 million dollars in 2017	Global: 190 countries
	Couchsurfing	About 14 million members	–	Global: 200,000 cities
Transport	**Uber**	3 million active drivers	20 billion gross bookings (2016)	Global: 600 cities in 58 countries
	Lyft	100,000 registered users	1.2 billion dollars in 2015	USA
	BlaBlaCar	60 million members	Estimated annual revenues of 72 million dollars	International: 22 countries
Catering	**EatWith**	20,000 hosts 150,000 guests	–	International: 130 countries
	BonAppetour	500 registered guests	–	International: 80 cities

Source: OECD, 2016 and companies' websites

The contemporary presence in the same market of businesses that are highly regulated and of others that are not is therefore creating an unfair competition scenario which must be reviewed quickly and adapted to new needs.

This issue is being raised in countless countries and no way has been found so far to achieving a transparent set of common rules that are identical for everyone. The response has been quite chaotic: in some cases highly restrictive rules have been adopted for the sharing economy while in others a more liberal attitude has prevailed, so as not to limit or even constrain the development of this important new sector.

The problem is not easy to solve for various reasons. Tourism is not a sector that is simple to categorise under the usual economic sectors. It is transversal to culture, to the environment, to agriculture, to infrastructures and, above all, to transport.

Moreover, in vertical terms, the sharing economy and tourism touch and encompass interests that are not exclusively national, but also exist at regional or local levels, those at which the most intense regulatory actions have occurred with the introduction of new, mainly punitive rules or, in any case, ones that tend to restrict the sharing economy.

In order to create an adequate regulatory framework as soon as possible, it is therefore crucial first of all for both new and traditional operators to be given the ability to carry out their activities in a transparent competitive context, and then to make it possible for new businesses to grow and develop.

The widest horizontal and vertical collaboration is necessary between the various levels of public organisation in order to achieve this, with the involvement of the sharing economy platforms and the different categories of operators in the tourism sector.

In the final analysis, this constitutes a unique opportunity for significantly streamlining the regulatory framework in force once and for all, as it is often no longer fit for the evolution of the market and for the full development of the tourism sector. Both the OECD[2] and the European Union have specifically commented in this spirit, the latter with the publication of specific guidelines aimed at all Member States. The indications emerging regard consumer protection and workers' rights in particular.

On the taxation front, the proposals tend towards the identification of more appropriate taxation levels on the basis of the transaction types. As regards the large commercial platforms, for example, they make a distinction between the small occasional operations by individuals and the activities of commercially-minded operators, while social platforms and those with a non-profit ethos are encouraged.

It is in this light that it is possible to view the model adopted by France and by other countries that assigns to the platforms themselves (e.g. Airbnb) the responsibility for collecting the tax liabilities for the transactions and, in some cases, the tourism tax where applicable. Also obligatory is for those who exceed certain annual thresholds to register in special tax registers, for example for renting houses.

Even though the establishment of new rules is being evaluated in many countries and some have already adopted new governance standards for the sector, the current situation in general is mainly one of *wait and see*.

In the meantime the sharing economy continues to grow in an effervescent manner and demands solutions.

It generates economic growth and new jobs, stimulates innovation and new experiences, creates new enterprises and spreads inclusive prosperity, especially in tourism. The fear that the sector limits or damages traditional business is exaggerated and unjustified. The available data seem to confirm that the business is substantially additional and only partly substitutive. This business is increasingly directing itself towards less familiar regions and destinations with only modest tourist structures and traditional services. It therefore tends to benefit new communities that are still off the beaten track and excluded from the great streams of tourists.

Faced with changes of this kind and scale, the entire operator chain must therefore update its proposals rapidly and adapt them to the new needs of travellers and of the tools that technological innovation has made available to everyone.

Notes

[1] PWC, 2016 http://www.pwc.co.uk/issues/megatrends/collisions/sharingeconomy/future-of-the-sharing-economy-in-europe-2016.html.

[2] See the 2016 study, *Policies for the Tourism Sharing Economy*, in "OECD Tourism Trends and Policies 2016", OECD Publishing.

6   From Giant Cruise Ships to the Bike: How Tourists of the Future Will Travel

The journey used to be considered the least interesting part of a holiday but with the passage of time we have realised that the hours and days spent reaching our destination could be transformed into something pleasant, interesting and worth considering to be an integral part of the holiday – or even the holiday itself as in the case of the Orient Express or cruise ships. It is obvious, moreover, that the transport system can be crucial for a destination's tourism success. Accessibility is one of the main sticking points that limit tourism and the problem is unquestionably linked to transport.

From a technical standpoint accessibility is intended as the ease (or lack of it) with which a given destination can be reached: i.e. the availability of links, their frequency, their cost and their intermodal organisation.

Southern Italy is an emblematic case of how accessibility can condition the tourist success of an area. Only 13% of international tourists visiting Italy travel south of Naples: why? Is it because these regions are less attractive? Are they poor in terms of landscape, nature and culture? Are they dear or cursed by the weather? Obviously not! Poor accessibility is the main factor that limits their development.

The availability and quality of a good road system is always a significant indicator of the level of development and, all things considered, of the quality of life in a region. And in fact its comparative measurement is one of the most important parameters used at international level for assessing a location's competitiveness. Networks of these infrastructures require enormous investments that are linked to their ability to generate wealth.

With numbers in constant growth and good future prospects it is tourism that is generating the demand behind new infrastructure and interconnection projects: motorways, railway lines and airports.

Until the 1980s, getting from one place to another could be quite complex, especially air travel which was fairly costly and offered far less availability than it does today. As a result, people preferred not to have to travel too far for their holidays. Tourism was mainly concentrated in Europe because – especially in the south – the great attractions of the localities bathed by the Mediterranean Sea acted as the catalyst, pulling in as much as 70% of world tourism (even today the figure well exceeds 50%).

The car was the preferred means of travel or, less frequently, the coach and train. Flying was scarcely used.

Then everything changed at the end of the 1990s. Until then the main airlines, known as "flag carriers", were state-owned: with little appetite for competition they were inefficient and very inattentive to the needs of consumer-travellers. Running costs were extremely high and so, therefore, were ticket prices. The small range of available flights were very expensive, with the same prices for all the companies and kept that way by cartel agreements.

Driven by the United States – where local airlines operated in free market conditions with real competition – Europe decided to adapt, and a true revolution took place. Many public companies were privatised and many of these closed shop and failed, creating incredible shocks such as in 2001 when Swissair ceased operations, a company that had for years constituted a benchmark for stability and quality service. The survivors had to record enormous losses, seek allies or merge with other companies. The free market imposed new rules, new dynamics, corporate restructuring, new routes and new fares.

This was also the period that saw the rise of low-cost airlines that were able to offer prices that were so cheap that they almost seemed impossible.

Not only did consumers learn to compare different companies' fares with greater attention, but also the fares themselves were no longer fixed as they had been in the past; instead they were now dynamic, i.e. they were different for early bookers and last-minute ones.

The arrival of the low-cost companies was also behind the development of "point to point" networks composed of routes between secondary, decentralised and cheaper airports; this meant that it was no longer necessary to break up journeys by having to transit through a capital or "hub", a major airport.

In just a few years, all of this, along with the development of charters, transformed aircraft from an exclusive means of transport for the few into a cheap handy option for the masses. Flight routes and destinations grew rapidly and we quickly learnt to recognise and desire new tourism locations – often far away – that became famous, familiar and successful. Destinations such as the Red Sea and Sharm el-Sheikh immediately became competitive vis-à-vis seaside destinations in the Mediterranean.

Making an incredible number of potential new tourism destinations accessible was truly revolutionary. Many countries immediately realised how important a focus on tourism could be for their development and for job creation, and competition stiffened immediately at global level: a new competitor could come onto the field every time a new route was inaugurated. This was the great fortune of the Maldives, the Caribbean and the islands of the Indian Ocean. Millions of tourists from Northern Europe found alternatives to the usual resorts and nothing remained as before.

During these same years, straddling 2000, the development of the airports was accompanied by the growth of online business with search engines that provided tourists with direct tools for obtaining information, comparisons and bookings that made it extremely fast and easy to decide and book.

Today air is the most popular means of transport with tourists, followed by land (road and rail) travel and water. This last sector, which may not seem very significant, actually includes a tourism component in rapid and continuous growth: the cruise. This activity has attracted great interest in the last 20 years, also thanks to sweeping product diversification, and numbers are rising continuously: according to the CLIA's (Cruise Lines International Association) 2018 Cruise Industry Outlook, from 2009 to 2018 cruise passengers have increased from 17.8 million to 27.2 million.

Figure 1   Mode of transport used for outbound trips worldwide

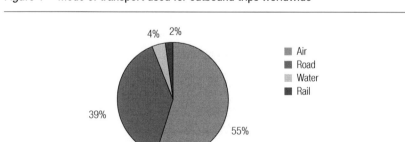

Source: Elaboration from UNWTO 2017 data

Though a great deal has changed in tourism is the last 10–15 years, we are again at the start of a new evolution which will see profound transformation of the sector and continue at least until 2030.

By 2030 the world's middle class will exceed 5 billion and as many as two-thirds of these will be international tourists, the majority of Asiatic origin, and they will mainly travel by plane. These are enormous numbers that will force the transport system to fund new solutions involving colossal investments: bigger and bigger aircraft and airports, mega hubs, new road networks, motorways, ports, ships and so on. A gigantic and complex global challenge with countless unknowns starting right from those linked to pollutant emissions.

What happens every day in the skies above our heads and how incredible the amount of air traffic actually is can be seen on YouTube in the amazing videos made by the NATS (National Air Traffic Services), one of the largest air traffic control agencies in the world.

These scenarios also underline the links between tourism, transport and sustainability, seen from the dual standpoint of carrying capacity and environmental sustainability.

Planes and cars, which as we have seen will be the most utilised means, are also the most polluting. The figures available provide a disturbing picture: tourism has a great environmental impact and therefore a great effort is required in this sector too to continue with the improvement of air quality, and the reduction of traffic and noise. At the moment there is no sight of any concrete solution to this challenge in the short term.

Without question airports will be at the centre of this challenge and many projects launched for their evolution already indicate the targets and results it is intended to obtain. The starting point is a simple observation of fact: today's international airport system is incapable of handling the 7 billion or so international and domestic passengers who are expected by 2030.

Beijing, for example, had to build a new airport to replace the current one which was only expanded in 2008 but was soon no longer able to absorb passenger growth. The new airport will become the world's largest airport serving 100 million passengers annually. And the same can be said of at least 20 international airports among the world's most important.

Extensions, but above all, changes that go well beyond the mere dimensional question: it is not just a simple matter of new and longer runways, or greater spaces for transiting and disembarking, but a change of perspective which will profoundly modify an extremely broad context involving the hinterland, town-planning, industrial settlements and the network of services, all the way to the very concept of airport itself: no longer simply a place that is simply dedicated to transfers but also to stays and much else.

The road has already been traced in a clear manner today: most international airports allocate most of their space to shops, restaurants and other commercial activities. To the point that for many of these airports the "non-aviation" business – in other words the income generated by commercial services intended for passengers, operators and visitors in the airports, not to mention the real estate activities – has already far exceeded the "aviation" part (services and activities linked to planes landing and taking off; ground-handling services; security services, etc.).

Heathrow Airport is a clear example of this evolution. 250 of the 300 most important companies currently operating in London have actually opted to establish their offices in the vicinity of the airport. Thanks to the infrastructural transport network which was extended and improved over the years, and to extraordinary territorial planning, Heathrow has become a very easy complex to reach and move from towards the rest of the world.

Alongside the shops and commercial activities in Heathrow – 70 outlets including Gucci, Bottega Veneta, Louis Vuitton, Chanel and over 40 restaurants – services to individuals, such as personal shoppers, spa treatments or areas dedicated to families and to mothers for breast-feeding and changing babies have been blossoming. And, of course, simple free Wi-Fi connections for everyone.

Furthermore, the airport offers and will increasingly offer links to the surrounding territory and first and foremost to the nearby urban centres, in order to speed up transfer times, reducing them to a minimum through a diversified intermodal air-car-taxi or air-rail network and with the maximum possible streamlining of customers and security-related procedures.

In this way, if on one hand the network of links between airport, hinterland, resident community, tourism, industrial and production networks will become increasingly complex, on the other it will establish the groundwork for new sites and not simply for new businesses but also for the widest tanging facilities such as stadiums, casinos, cinemas and, of course basic airport services such as car parks and hotels.

In short, the great international airports of the future will increasingly be new multifunctional structures in a metropolitan context, ones that are

Figure 2   The development of air traffic from 2016 to 2035

2016	from 2016 to 2035	2035
• 55 Aviation Megacities*	• 33,000 aircraft required	• 95 Aviation Megacities
• 3.5 billion passengers	• 4.5% passenger traffic growth p.a.	• 7 billion passengers
• 25% of the emerging economies population took a trip in 2016	• 500,000 new pilots	• 75% of the emerging economies population will take a trip in 2035
	• Domestic PRC will be the biggest traffic flow within the next 10 years	• 2.5 million daily passengers (long-haul traffic to/from/ via Megacities)

*Aviation Megacities: Cities with more than 10,000 daily long-haul passengers (flight distance >
2,000 nm excluding domestic traffic)
Source: Airbus Global Market Forecast, 2016

capable of attacting the widest-ranging interests and are less and less dependent on the strict aviation component, and that offer opportunities for
creating wealth and employment in a relational scenario that is radically
different from the current one.

If much has changed for air transport, the same must be expected for
car use. How will we build our roads, motorways and towns to absorb an
increase in cars on the scale of the one foreseeable from the growth in
population and tourism?

We already know that it will not be easy and probably impossible to
construct new viability structures and that therefore we will have to find
new ways of getting around. Today, most cars only have one occupant and
are used for less than two hours per day. As a result, 20% of the ground in
cities is occupied semi-permanently by parked vehicles.

Science and technology are studying new solutions and countless projects and applications are already available and promising look: from the
hybrid and electric motors which will soon be available to replace traditional petrol or diesel internal combustion engines, to driverless vehicles
that are capable of following routes of all kinds and which, when available,
will be able to revolutionise the way we travel by car.

Box 1   Uber and new private car transport

As often happens in human history it is actually the most banal events that trigger the greatest discoveries. Innovation has always been the result of the challenge that humanity has with itself, to improve the status quo and its own limits.

In the case of Uber the banal event occurred on a cold December night in far-off 2008. Two young men, Travis Kalanick and Garrett Camp, were in Paris to attend the LeWeb conference. At the end of a long day they decided to go home but because of the late hour, combined with the onset of a snowfall, they couldn't find even one car to take them back. For far too long they stood in the road watching cars streaking past in the direction that they should have been taking: "if only I could have pressed a button and have a car all for myself, now that I need one." So simple an observation as to even appear facile, but the challenge that came from it certainly was not the case.

Today Uber is present in over 600 cities and 70 countries and has bypassed the threshold of 5 billion trips worldwide by people who can access a vehicle to get around wherever they are with one simple click.

Among the things for which Uber is particularly appreciated by travellers are the ease of use of the app and the possibility of paying directly by credit card with the app so that it is not necessary to travel with lots of cash and perhaps with different currencies.

Notwithstanding the debates triggered by the introduction of the service in different countries, related to the very aggressive policies of the company, the regulation of the service and the protection of workers, there is no denying that, today, the technology underlying Uber provides answers that go well beyond the burgeoning mobility needs of people all over the world and tackles a need for transparency, safety, reliability and simplicity which are indispensable and which this new type of service is able to offer.

Of course much will depend not only on the price of petrol but also on the decisions of governments and on their ability to incentivise and orientate consumption patterns, on the rules that local administrations will produce to limit traffic in town centres and on the regulations which will gradually come into force governing safety and pollution, as well as on town planning and on new spaces created for cycle lanes for example.

It is highly probable that, while the use of private vehicles will be progressively constrained, the network of public ground and, where possible, underground services will be fostered and upgraded. An important contribution is also given by the car-sharing services that are already available in a great many cities and also the new private car transport services that will also contribute to channelling consumption habits towards shared car use.

Bicycles are also experiencing a comeback in a great many cities around the world. The bicycle is the ideal means for the future – and the bike of the future will be an extremely light and foldable one that can interact with smartphone apps or other wearables in order to monitor physical activity – because it is cheap, sustainable, healthy and easy to use and because more than any other means it lets us rediscover rhythms and a relationship with our surrounding environment.

Tourists also love bikes and, especially in recent years, they have rediscovered the bicycle in combination with trains and with boats on rivers and canals. This is particularly true in Europe where new itineraries specifically designed for travellers have been created, and where there has also been huge growth in the market for electric or e-bikes.

A 2012 study of the European Cycle Route Network, EuroVelo, estimated that about 2.3 billion cycling trips were undertaken in Europe with an economic impact on the localities of about 44 billion euros.

In France thousands cycle along the 800 km trails of the Loire Valleys, with it castles, while the cycling economy in Germany is worth 6 billion euros including bike-hotels, shops and workshops. But cycling tourism has also been highly successful in North America, in South Africa and in Australia, just to mention a few.

Cycling has enormous growth potential and the bearer of countless benefits. The World Health Organization estimates that it is possible to save over 100 billion dollars in health costs and 3 billion dollars in reduced pollution through greater bike use around the globe.

Will all this be enough? We hope so, but it is probable that more will be needed. It is not possible to buy a private car in some Northern European cities today unless you are able to show that you have a dedicated parking place.

Perhaps we will soon have to face up to the end of certain ways of living with the automobile that had a very different role, an importance and sense for past generations, also as regards tourism, that are very different from those it will have for our children and grandchildren.

In 1908, the American author Edith Wharton, travelling in France with her husband, wrote: "The motor-car has restored the romance of travel. Freeing us from all the compulsions and contacts of the railway, the bondage to fixed hours and the beaten track, the approach to each town through the area of ugliness and desolation created by the railway itself, it has given us back the wonder, the adventure and the novelty which enlivened the way of our posting grandparents."[1]

These words are perfectly comprehensible for the Belle Époque but no longer reflect the reality for millions of people who are often trapped in mega jams during holiday weekends.

Some help will come in the future from the train, another means of transport with a marked sustainable vocation and with enormous potential for growth, both for short and medium–long distance, thanks to new technologies and the upgrading of old lines and rolling stock but especially from high-speed trains.

Thanks to this it will be easier and easier to replace planes with trains, already competitive today both from the economic standpoint and for journeys up to 500/600 km long.

A good example of this evolution is the Milan–Rome route in Italy which was a real cash cow for Alitalia for decades up to the early 2000s as the airline operated a virtual monopoly for air transport between the two cities. Then, with the introduction of a new high-speed rail service, air inexorably lost competitiveness to the point that the route is no longer of interest to the low-cost companies which had previously been attempting with little luck to break the monopoly of what was then the flag carrier.

Even from a tourist standpoint the train should therefore be seen today as a particularly interesting and competitive means, also because of intermodality with the plane and for reaching town centres from the airports.

The huge investments already in the pipeline in this sector clearly indicate that between now and 2030 the train will revolutionise the way we travel, to the benefit of sustainability and the quality of our journeys.

However, train does not and will not simply mean high speed because, thanks to people's desire to discover regions in new ways and tourists' pursuit of special experiences, this old means is witnessing a successful revival and there great expectations for growth even on minor sections. Greater sensitivity towards the environment and landscape, a new desire for knowledge of our surroundings, and the pursuit of slower rhythms away from the stresses of everyday life have led us to the redisovery and appreciation of local and historic trains: slow but capable of plunging us into valleys and woods, amid localities and mountains that would otherwise by difficult to reach. For a kind of tourism that makes the journey itself an integral and significant holiday experience.

As a result, many secondary lines, often forgotten – or worse still, abandoned – are coming back to life. The French, Swiss, Austrian or Italian Alps have provided the ideal lands for trialling this type of tourism which is gradually spreading to many other territories, hand in hand and in synergy with food and wine tourism, agriculture, with local cultural attractions, popular holidays and traditions, and especially with the bicycle.

Just one example, so glorious that it was declared a UNESCO World Heritage Site in 2008, and needs to be booked well in advance, is the Bernina Express, the red train that links Chur/Davos/St. Moritz/Valposchiavo/Tirano.

Finally, a few words on water transport, the lion's share of which continues to be held by cruising, at least judging by the many ships under construction and which will take to the seas in the coming years: giants over 360 m long with 18 bridges that will be able to carry up to 6,780 passengers and 2,100 crew members such as *Symphony of the Seas* (Royal Caribbean).

These ships will increasingly seek out their markets in the Pacific and in the eastern seas in line with tourism expectations. The case of cruising is perhaps and emblematically the most obvious example of how to transform the journey itself, the component that was once considered the least interesting part of the holiday, into an enthralling, essential and even unmissable experience.

In conclusion, efficient, interconnected and sustainable mobility is at the basis of future prosperity and hopefully can be achieved as soon as possible in order to satisfy both the tourism that will grow considerably in the coming years and especially in order to reduce the environmental impact that this sector produces.

The target for the coming decades is to be able to move and travel more rapidly and easily, thanks to new infrastructures and to digital and technological innovations. However we will have to learn how to behave in a more intelligent, aware and sustainable manner while doing without some things but improving the quality of our lives.

Note

[1] Edith Wharton, *A Motor-Flight through France*, New York, Scribner, 1908, p. 1.

7   Space Tourists

From trains to transatlantic liners, from the car to the plane, huge advances made in transport have carried us further and made very remote locations feel closer and more accessible, as tourists too. This progress does not, indeed almost never, spring from factors linked to the expansion of leisure tourism but rather arises for commercial and business reasons, or military ones.

But people are always dreaming and pushing their imagination towards the unknown. And so it was at the end of the 1960s too.

On 21 December 1968, three men – Frank Borman, James Lovell and William Anders – left the Earth on board *Apollo 8* to reach the Moon for the first time and orbit it. At Christmas that year they gifted humanity with the stunning picture of the terrestrial dawn, 700 lunar photographs, images and observations on the hidden side of the Moon accompanied by the live commentary of the three astronauts as they gazed upon the "blue planet" from a distance of over 300,000 km.

A few months later, on 20 July 1969, Neil Armstrong and Buzz Aldrin, accompanied by millions of viewers glued to the TV, made the first steps on the Moon and brought home a dream, above all, and then 22 kg of lunar samples.

From then on, travelling in space seemed like an enterprise within the grasp of us all to the point that up to 1971 Pan Am, spurred by the demand for space tourism, actually issued over 93,000 "First Moon Flights" vouchers, booking cards numbered in order of priority for the first moon flight.

As things turned out, no tourist got to space but the vouchers have become collectors' items and they can be found today in museums like the Science Museum in London or sold at auctions.

Figure 1   Pan American Airways (Pan Am) "First Moon Flights" Club membership
              card

This is because the dream of citizen space exploration slowly faded away
in the 1970s: if sending a man to Mars seemed the most obvious development at the end of the 1960s after the conquest of the Moon, during
the 1970s and '80s the contraction of public expenditure for space pro-
grammes, the suppression of the Apollo programme, the launch of the
space shuttle programme and the age of the orbiting International Space
Station (ISS, 1984) ended up by imprisoning man in the earth's orbit. At
least until the present day.

Now, in the new millennium, space tourism is being discussed again.
Why?

The reasons are many and various: one that can be identified from an
economic standpoint is the growing presence of, and competition between, market operators in the aerospace sector, triggered by the policies
of international government agencies. In particular, NASA has passed
progressively from a government-managed system of access to the ISS to
a competitive system in which the goods transport operations are provided by private companies with fixed-price contracts (Commercial Orbital
Transportations Services). This has triggered a race towards technological
innovation with a view to lowering the costs for the costs of launch vehicles, for the construction of efficient space vehicles and for recovering and
reusing the first stages of the rockets.

Figure 2 Space tourism and its implications

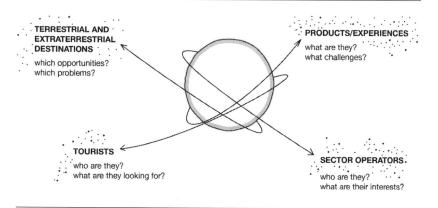

Low-cost access to space is in fact a fundamental requirement and driving factor for the development of mankind's exploration of space. The stakes are very high and only partly linked to tourism as exploitation of the natural and energy resources of the bodies nearest to the Earth is also involved; the possibility of constructing extraterrestrial human colonies; the important fallout in terms of technological and scientific innovation that space research has for other economic sectors from telecommunications to medicine and finally the knock-on effect of aerospace-linked investments for local economies.

For this reason, from the point of view of development of the sector, rather than real space tourism, it would perhaps be correct to speak of the development of space technology for leisure and entertainment purposes as part of the broader phenomenon of the privatisation of the space industry.

But what is space tourism today and what implications does it have?

The topic can be analysed from at least four closely connected points of view: the products and the experiences under development or already available on the market; the economic operators involved; the demand; the opportunities for the regions and destinations on Planet Earth (Figure 2).

1. Tourism in space: products and operators

In recent years we have become accustomed to great announcements of imminent space journeys: these generate a certain enthusiasm, mainly associated with technological and engineering evolution linked to this sector.

Only about 500 people have been to space at the time of writing of this book and only ten or so can really be described as tourists. The experience enjoyed by this handful of people was a stay in the International Space Station where a visitor was hosted for the first time in 2001 when the businessman Dennis Tito stayed for seven days, orbiting the Earth at a height of 400 km and at 27,000 km/h for about $20 million.

2.   Orbital tourism

What these tourists go through is essentially what astronauts experience during their missions on the ISS. Reaching the station cost them millions of dollars and intense preparation both for launching into orbit on by Soyuz capsule and for adapting to life in space: discomfort, permanency in spaces with a maximum diameter of 4.5 m, basically designed for scientific research purposes, dawns and sunsets every 45 minutes and so on. Such tourism is not for everyone, from all standpoints: physical, mental and economic.

However many companies today are developing new technologies and new services conceived for orbital tourism with designs of the spaces and services specifically intended for citizen space exploration. Indeed the latter actually constitutes an important area in what NASA calls "LEO (Low Earth Orbit) commercialization", all the more so considering the fact that the ISS itself will have to be decommissioned between 2024 and 2028 and it will therefore be able/have to find new uses.

Bigelow Aerospace, for example, a company founded by the American hotelier, Robert Bigelow, has developed "Expandable Activity Modules" for the ISS which could also be employed for the space hotels of the future and, in 2018, Orion Span, another important US aerospace business, announced the construction of the first luxury space hotel by 2022. Orion Span will use the Aurora Station for this enterprise. This is a space module that is 10 m long and 4.2 m wide that will be able to host up to four people and two crew members for 12 days at 320 km above the Earth. Price: $9.5 million.

The costs of this type of tourism, in its next evolutions too, will remain extremely high for many years to come, even if companies like SpaceX and Boeing are investing billions of dollars to create cheaper systems for

Figure 3 "Deployable Modular Frame technology applied to an Inflatable commercial space station"

Source: courtesy Vittorio Netti

transporting both astronauts and civilians – not to mention goods – to the International Space Station.

3. Sub-orbital tourism

A lot cheaper, and therefore potentially accessible to a larger public on the other hand, is the growing market for sub-orbital tourism, with many operators vying for conquest. Among these, Virgin Galactic and Blue Origin in particular have achieved great prominence not only with their feats, highly publicised by the media, but also because of the visibility of their founders, Richard Branson and Jeff Bezos respectively.

Virgin Galactic aims to offer the thrill of microgravity on its Space-ShipTwo-class spaceplane, VSS *Unity*. For a figures of about $250,000 passengers will be able to experience weightlessness for about 6 minutes while gazing at the curvature of the earth standing out against the darkness of space.

Blue Origin, on the other hand, has successfully tested its Crew Capsule 2.0, launched by a New Shepard reusable booster rocket, designed to carry a six-member crew for a sub-orbital flight of about 7 minutes beyond the

Kármán line, i.e. the boundary between the Earth's atmosphere and outer space. The large windows of the capsule are designed to allow passengers to get the most stunning views of the Earth as they float weightlessly for a few minutes.

The question that we must ask at this point, at least from a tourist perspective, is whether we can really consider sub-orbital trips to be tourism.

And this for various reasons. From a definition standpoint, tourism implies at least one overnight stay in a destination. The duration of suborbital trips is limited and the destination doesn't really exist as the tourist leisure activity is mixed up with the transport component.

What the experience really entails it the ability to board a space vehicle, arrive in orbit, stay there for a few minutes while enjoying new sensations and views and then return to the Earth. There are not many comparisons with present forms of tourism in which the transport component – though an integral part of the travel experience – is primarily just for getting from one place to another.

Even if space travel is often compared to aviation – also in terms of evolutionary possibilities – in reality the most appropriate comparison from a strictly tourism viewpoint is perhaps with cruising as this is the only form of tourism in which the destination loses its centrality in favour of the experience on board and the view of outer space from afar. Also similar is the role of the tourists themselves which is very much under the control of others in this type of trip as they lose their freedom of movement and choice.

Another totally original factor that distinguishes sub-orbital tourism from tourism as we know it today is the fleetingness of the interaction between tourists and the landscape that interests them, an interaction that has been defined by some scholars as the "kinematics" of perception and touch. This fleetingness transforms this type of experience into a profoundly commercial product which will require original strategies in order to maintain great interest on the demand side, if it is to maintain a sufficiently exciting overlap between transport and leisure for a vast market.

4.   Circumnavigation and point-to-point tourism

Many of these uncertainties will be resolved in what tourism to other celestial bodies might turn out to be, to the Moon first of all, but also Mars and its moons, Phobos and Deimos.

Journeys to other planets will naturally rebalance the relationship between journey and tourism, between tourist and destination, moving it to a dimension that is more forcefully embedded in our desire for exploration and knowledge.

Though marketing this type of tourism experience is not envisaged anytime soon, scientific and technological research and competition between operators is very lively.

In 2017 Elon Musk's SpaceX had announced that in 2018 it would be ready to take two paying tourists on a circumnavigation of the Moon lasting a week, using the *Falcon Heavy* rocket. However it then postponed the enterprise, also so as to concentrate its resources on the construction of the *Big Falcon Rocket* (BFR), a super space vehicle with a height of 106 m and width of 9 capable of reaching the Moon and Mars, complete with a capsule for a crew of 40.

This fascinating enterprise, reported by the media worldwide, has already generated countless declarations of interest from potential multi-millionaire tourists.

Nevertheless this type of undertaking requires the solution of countless problems: these are not simply linked to the costs and development of the technology but also relate to the extremely high safety standards envisaged for manned missions, the potential negative effects on the human body and mind (radiation, loss of muscular mass, osteoporosis, claustrophobia and much more), the design and development of the spaces and services for comfort when cruising and staying in the space capsules, regulating the use of the available space and definition of the insurance tools for passengers, to mention but a few.

5.   The demand for space tourism

What has been described so far provides a snapshot of the development of citizen space exploration but it has quite clearly not yet taken the form of full-blown space tourism.

But also of central importance are the potential tourists themselves: will the demand be sufficient to sustain the development of the sector? Who will the space tourists be and what will they really see? Will they be content with a glimpse of the Earth's curvature or will they demand the tangible sensation of leaving a dusty footprint on the Moon? Who of us will want to and have the physical and economic resources to tackle an experience of this kind?

Answering these questions is quite complex: real market surveys have so far mainly been carried out on sub-orbital flights which, for the moment, are the only space tourism product that is potentially accessible to a large – though very well-to-do – number of people. Furthermore, the estimates made over time have never really been able to use any real flight start dates as a reference as these have been put back continually.

Some market surveys had already been done at the beginning of the 2000s (Futron Corporation, 2002) and others followed between 2010 and 2012 (Astrium/Ipsos; Tauri Group) but not only have they always led to very different results but they have been hard to compare, also because of the different ways the interviews were carried out and because of the potential consumers' lack of knowledge of the product, especially in terms of the riskiness and type of experience.

Nevertheless, demand always exceeded the envisaged supply, even in the worst scenarios. Many of these surveys focussed on the American and Asian markets, but the European Commission also carried out several studies of the subject (Strategy&) using its Eurobarometers (403) to gauge the interest of European citizens for space tourism.

The picture changes for potential clients for space missions to the Moon and Mars: given the extremely high investment costs, the main goal for the companies currently involved in this market is still to attract multi-millionaire investors who are space enthusiasts and who are prepared to invest in the enterprise in order to obtain "first fly" guarantees.

For everyone else, the not-so-wealthy, there is nevertheless an entire industry that is ready to offer the key elements of the space experience at accessible prices: the view of the Earth's curvature, parabolic flights at zero-G or astronaut training like that organised by the National Aerospace Training and Research (NASTAR) in the USA. You can experience authentic NASA-style training on a shuttle simulator, a journey to Mars or an Earth orbit at the Epcot Future World of the Walt Disney World Resort in Orlando.

And then, at home, we can always explore the lunar landing sites free of charge and participate in virtual lunar tours using Google Moon.

Box 1   Archaeological tourism on the Moon

In addition to the experience of the means of transport and weightlessness, central to both orbital and sub-orbital tourism is the exceptional view of the Earth: a chance to admire the succession of blue expanses of ocean, of the terrestrial masses and of the deserts from a unique perspective against the background of the black universe.

But by the time that the first tourists are able to set foot on other planets, on the Moon or on Mars, the centre of interest will inevitably have shifted to these destinations. So what will the tourists see and what will they be looking for?

It is not difficult to imagine that, after the first impact with such different environments and once they have recovered from the amazement and thrill of the trip, they will go looking for the traces of those who had already explored these places physically or by robot.

The sites of the six Apollo moon landings retain countless traces of man's passage and are still of great scientific and historical significance.

Three Apollo sites are actually still scientifically active and all the landing sites provide means for learning about changes caused by the long-term exposure of man-made systems to the lunar environment: food, paints, plastic, rubber, metals and so on. Such data are of great scientific interest which cannot be found elsewhere.

But aside from the research aspects, the Moon still conserves symbolic testimony of man's passage: flags, family photographs, footprints, impressions on the ground and historic objects such as the Goodwill Disk, a thin silica disc on which greetings from leaders of 73 of the world's nations were etched at a microscopic scale.

Figure 4   A family photography of the astronaut Charles Duke (*Apollo 16*) left on the lunar surface, and the impression of the astronaut's boot.

Source: NASA

For its future visitors the Moon provides an attraction that no other celestial body can offer: "archaeological parks" of the first human presence in space.
In fact any traces on Mars are only mechanical.
And so, in July 2011, in the certainty that the landing sites and terrestrial artefacts on the Moon will be fundamental poles of attraction for future expeditions, NASA issued a protocol drafted by a Lunar Historic Site (LHS) team for the conservation of the human traces and artefacts in them.
The document was the result of a great conceptual effort for differentiating the statute of the objects and for delineating study and protective strategies, but also for establishing a territorial right, however circumscribed, around the objects belonging to the government of the United States that are still present on lunar soil.*
This document's recommendations were then further reinforced in the report, "Protecting & Preserving Apollo Program Lunar Landing Sites & Artefacts" published by the United States Government in March 2018.

* Stefano Catucci, *Imparare dalla Luna*.

6.   Opportunities for regions on the Earth

Any trip into space today must inevitably start from the Earth. Perhaps one day it will not be so and we will be able to book a room on Mars and reach a Martian station directly from our lunar base, but for the moment the space tourism game will be played in terrestrial spaceports.

Just as the touristic and economic development of regions is based on the presence of efficient and well-connected transport and intermodality infrastructures, so will it be too for space tourism which will require functional hubs.

Such hubs are essentially complex systems of suitable physical and technological structures for launching sub-orbital craft and missile boosters, and their presence constitutes an extraordinary opportunity for the regions in which they are situated in terms of induced economic activity and place branding, of commercial and industrial opportunities and also of technological development. In many cases, in fact, the areas around spaceports are also areas with important industrial and aerospace poles that are able to supply the products and services required for the take-off, launch, maintenance and assembly activities.

The positioning of spaceports does not however simply follow economic and industrial criteria but also geographical ones: this is because rockets can reach satellite orbits more easily if launched close to the equator, thereby maximising the use of the Earth's rotation speed.

The first spaceport to be designed and built specifically for commercial use was Spaceport America. In the Jornada del Muerto desert, it was inaugurated in 2011 by the governor of New Mexico in the presence of Richard Branson, president of Virgin Galactic, which will manage the sub-orbital flights. Branson also signed an agreement in 2018 for creating a new spaceport in Italy at Grottaglie, one of the main Italian and European aerospace districts.

8 Tourism as a Creative Industry

Culture in the broadest sense has always been one of the great themes of the tourism conversation. A great deal has been said about tourism linked to cities of art, to exhibitions, to museums, to archaeology, to UNESCO heritage sites and to major events such as the European Capitals of Culture: in particular in relation to the debate on the instruments for exploiting cultural assets for regional development, and regarding sustainability themes.

In fact cultural tourism is often considered by administrators and scholars as a panacea, one that is potentially more accessible and qualitatively superior to other forms of tourism.

Accessible to all destinations because, while it is not possible to develop seaside tourism where there is no sea, or mountain tourism where there are no mountains, there is culture everywhere; if adequately promoted and endowed with the minimum services necessary, even a destination with few significant artistic attractors can position itself on the cultural tourism map by staging exhibitions, events, specialised festivals or other similar initiatives.

And then it is qualitatively better as cultural tourism is unquestionably less seasonal than others, i.e. it is less concentrated in brief periods of the year because cultural tourists are generally associated with a higher spending capacity and greater attention and respect for the places they visit and, finally, because focussing on cultural tourism implies greater attention to conservation and appreciation of heritage.

Both these characteristics are clearly debatable.

As regards the former, it could be objected that on a visit to the United Arab Emirates, where the temperature can be 40 degrees in the shade, it is possible to ski at Ski Dubai for just €70 per day and encounter real penguins along the way. Today, technology also makes it possible to surf in Noth Wales at Surf Snowdonia, a jewel resulting from the joint effort of a leading cableway manufacturer (Leitner) and the Spanish company Wavegarden, which specialises in artificial waves.

Creativity, investments and marketing can therefore partly replace the gifts of nature, not only for developing cultural tourism but also sport and spa tourism, etc. On the other hand, there are hundreds of thousands of destinations with conspicuous cultural assets that are unable to take off touristically.

While it is generally possible to agree with the second property of cultural tourism – that it is qualitatively better (greater spending capacity of tourists and less seasonal flows), this view is partly contradicted by the state in which some cities of art, assailed by mass tourism, can be found. Two emblematic cases are Venice and Barcelona which have also been the subject of exposé documentaries, *The Venice Syndrome* and *Bye Bye Barcelona*, as well as of campaigns to raise awareness. Centres on a smaller scale include Cortona in Italy (also the subject of a documentary, *The Genius of a Place*) or Mont-Saint-Michel in France.

The problems with these destinations are obviously too multifaceted to be set out in full here. They pose complex challenges in policy terms as regards harmoniously integrating the development of tourism with that of other economic sectors and minimising environmental and social impacts on the territory and its residents. It is clear in fact that in some intensely and iconic cultural destinations, tourism can trigger processes that degrade the place's quality to the point that their very survival is threatened.

These assessments must then go hand in hand with an overall assessment of what cultural tourism effectively is today and on trends in the demand. In the sense that changes in demand can offer ideas for reconsidering the term *cultural*, intended not only as visiting museums and monuments, but also as enjoyment of the contemporary.

Cultural tourists are in fact an evolving species, no longer interested exclusively in museums and monuments, but also on the lookout for new ways of experiencing culture.

We have already suggested what they are looking for: products with typical identities perceived as authentic, experiences in which they themselves play an active, co-creative role, contact with residents, shopping for broadening horizons and learning and experimenting in an engaging manner.

Figure 1   Poster for the documentary *Bye Bye Barcelona* (2014) by Eduardo Chibás.

This mutation has been identified by the British scholar, Greg Richards, as *creative tourism*, namely a sort of post-cultural tourism in which tourists' preferences and roles change; but the types of cultural research are also multiplying and the very concept of culture is broadening: not just art, monuments and archaeology, but also festivals, events, contemporary art, architecture, fashion, design and crafts.

This is the way visitors to Delft not only familiarise themselves with Vermeer, but they also get to known about painting tiles; or pilgrims on the Via Francigena want to experience the real life of medieval travellers, sleeping on straw mattresses and eating dishes from the 13th century. Or on a trip to Scotland, tourists can identify themselves with the heroic figure of Robert the Bruce and take part in Scotland's first war of independence (1274–1329) in the interactive Battle of Bannockburn Museum.

The great success from the early 2000s of theme parks – intended as complex spectacular places of historical reconstruction and entertainment-learning such as Puy du Fou in the Vendée region of western France (2.3 million visitors yearly) or Warwick Castle in England (800,000 visitors) – and of museums that are increasingly interactive, featuring playful learning, is a further result of this trend which not only relates to Europe but also – and in an extremely evident manner – Asia: according to reports published by TEA/AECOM,[1] the top 20 parks in the Asia-Pacific region welcomed over 134 million people in 2017; the first 20 European parks hosted 62.6 million visitors, more than the population of Italy in other words. This component of the cultural and creative experience is increasingly characterising not only cultural tourism in the narrowest sense but is also sought in other segments such as the congress sector. Even shoppers are recording increasing interest not only in making purchases as such but

Box 1 Creative industries, social quality and economic development

According to the definition of Britain's Department of Culture, Media and Sport (2001),* creative industries are "those industries which have their origin in individual creativity, skill and talent and which have a potential for wealth and job creation through the generation and exploitation of intellectual property". Moreover, creative industries include "advertising, architecture, the art and antiques market, crafts, design, designer fashion, film and video, interactive leisure software, music, the performing arts, publishing, software and computer services, television and radio". Starting from the mid-1990s, the economic value generated by the creative goods and services production industries and the potential growth of the macro-sector compared to other economic ones has turned the spotlight onto the creative economy and driven the systemisation of knowledge of this macro sector.

This attention, starting from the English-speaking world, spread quickly to all the advanced economies and to the developing countries during the 2000s, with the creation of a global debate and giving life to a myriad of studies intended to delimit and quantify the creative economy: not an easy task given the considerable dynamism and variety of the industries that characterise it. Moreover, many international organisations like UNESCO, the United Nations Educational, Scientific and Cultural Organization, the United Nations Conference on Trade and Development, UNCTAD, the United Nations Conference on Trade and Development, and the UNDP – the United Nations Development Programme – have joined the debate, dedicating important surveys, publications and programmatic documents to the creative economy both in an attempt to quantify world trade in creative goods and services, and to present their own institutional viewpoints on the subject.

According to the European Parliament's report on EU policy for cultural and creative industries (2016), in Europe cultural and creative industries provide more than 12 million full-time jobs (7.5 % of the EU's work force), creating approximately 509 billion in value added to GDP but in specific regions, creative industries represent a significantly higher percentage of GDP and employ a higher percentage of the local workforce.

* See, Department for Culture, Media and Sport, *Creative Industries Mapping*, DCMS, 2001.

also, for example, in visits to the places of manufacture, participating in the production process, etc.

How can we satisfy these needs? How can we renew/complete traditional artistic-cultural products? How can new destinations be created? How can tourism be used to benefit the production and promotion of contemporary culture, and at the same time lighten the pressure on an overloaded artistic heritage?

If we shift our attention from demand to supply, we will see that some of the most interesting answers to these questions come today from the intersectoral interaction between the tourism industry and the system of creative enterprises.

Starting from the first decade of the 2000s interest has therefore been growing in the joint analysis of the creative industries macro sector in relation to tourism by entities such as the OECD which, in 2014, published a study entitled "Tourism and the Creative Economy", the European Commission and the regional and local governments which have allocated fresh resources to encourage opportunities for operational collaboration between creative industries and tourism.

The attention of tourism towards the cultural and creative industries actually includes at least three areas which, when working in synergy, can activate what the culture economist Walter Santagata,[2] called "Creative Atmosphere".

The first area regards the contribution that the creative industries make and can make to a destination's attractiveness. The second regards the role that creative enterprises can play in the construction of new tourism services by producing and supplying intermediate goods and services. Finally, the third is linked to possible synergies for promotion/marketing and for stimulating tourist spending.

Level 1. Creative industries, place branding and territorial attractiveness

The first level of interaction between tourism and creative industries refers to an area's attractiveness: creative industries contribute, sometimes crucially, to a place's offer and to attracting tourist flows. This is evident even only from a rapid analysis of the value propositions on the portals of the tourism boards of many countries in Europe and at international level. Products and services linked to creativity and, more broadly, to "made in" branding, are in the forefront of many of them: from the fine food and

wine system to architecture, from design to cinema, and from live entertainment to the videogame industry.

Design and architecture, to mention two important creative industries,
are sources of appeal for the Scandinavian countries. This is particularly
so for Sweden and Denmark where the tourism bodies have managed to
effectively exploit dedicated thematic itineraries through culture, creativity and shopping. Design is an extremely important touristic lever in
Italy too, as in the case of Milan's design week, for example. When we
examine the various creative industries – though they may be very different from one another in terms of business structure and of the goods
and services produced – we can appreciate just how much each of these
participates in some way to the characterisation of localities and to making them attractive.

Cinema attracts flows with festivals – from Berlin to Venice, from
Cannes to Locarno in Switzerland – and especially thanks to film tourism and to the productions attracted by national film boards: cinematic
phenomena such as *Star Wars: the Last Jedi* and *Star Wars: The Force Awak-
ens* or TV series like *Inspector Montalbano* have brought hundreds of film
crews operators to areas of Ireland and Sicily respectively, with a marked
increase in tourist flows in the regions and significant economic impacts.

Much is also made today of the potential contribution of the videogame
industry to tourism as various countries also seek to exploit their game
industries for tourism purposes: e.g. Finland which also promotes itself as
the "Angry Birds' Nest".

Other places are focussing on creativity associated with gastronomy,
working to consolidate systems that integrate the excellence of their raw
materials, their unique characteristics, scientific research linked to gastronomy and cultural development with international events, contemporary art and architecture and the achievement of various types of international recognition such as that of UNESCO designation as a Creative City
for Gastronomy. Others still focus on fashion.

At times the creative industries offer much more than an element of
attraction and become substitute components of a place's identity and fundamental part of place branding strategies. Examples include iconic architectural projects such as the Ciudad de las Artes y las Ciencias (1996) for
Valencia or the Cité des Civilisations du Vin in Bordeaux (2016), fashion
for Paris, design for Milan, cinema and *The Lord of the Rings* for New
Zealand.

One result of the pulling power of creative industries is also the growth in tourism in production districts. This is pushing many businesses and many "made in" localities to establish tourism services or company museums and visitor centres, and the effort to reconcile the activities and production times with those for hosting tourists is often quite considerable.

Many other destinations are preparing themselves for the construction of integrated supply systems that are linked to creativity and to the creative industries: this is the case, for example, with cities like Leipzig or Wolfsburg, with initiatives such as Creative Austria[3] or Creative Paris,[4] the "made in Italy" production and food and wine district initiatives such as Toscana Wine Architecture that suggests itineraries for discovering wine-linked architecture.

Level 2. Supply chain relationships

Creative industries are not just something that is immediately evident and touristically exploitable. They actually make an important contribution by offering intermediate goods and services to the tourism industry in a B2B framework and they feed the innovation processes.

Mention has been made in the previous paragraphs of how local products and creative services, culture and lifestyle have become central elements of the tourism experience, as shown in Figure 2.

This centrality of creative industries for the construction of tourist products and services develops in a network of collaborations between the two sectors, as more or less understood.

This was the case, for example, for the hospitality sector. The hotel industry and the entire non-hotel hospitality sector have been tackling a root and branch overhaul of their services in recent years. This has not simply involved a rethink of the business models following the development of online booking, disintermediation and the arrival of the sharing economy: since the 2000 the hospitality sector has become a test lab for experiential design, service design, for the design experience, for architecture, for technology and for new combinations with fashion, crafts and much else.

The "hotel" and "design"/"hotel and fashion" coupling has shown itself to be strategic both for relaunching the concept of hospitality, and for creating new opportunities for intervention and research for architects and designers, as can be seen from the investments made by various fashion brands in hotels.

Figure 2 Creativity and creative experiences in tourism framework

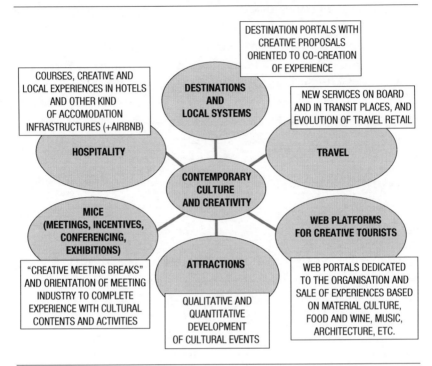

The entry of the great fashion houses into the world or hotel is a response, of course, to strategic category extension and brand positioning decisions which do not really have so much to do with tourism, but nevertheless constitute an interesting example of the relationship between two sectors, as can be seen from the experiences of Bulgari, Armani, Versace and other brands.

There is no shortage of occasions on the design and contemporary art front for collaboration with hotels and hostels and with the outdoor and the glamping sector. This is thanks both to the elements of stylistic innovation – and therefore of the repositioning that design injects into the hospitality world – and for reasons linked to new trends in sustainable planning and low-budget hospitality.

Design, art and fashion are not just exemplificative as there are evident contributions to tourism from other creative industries: from the fine food and wine industry to crafts, and from architecture to interior design.

The collaboration between the food and wine industry and the architectural one is favouring the extension of wine tourism to a broader public of cultural tourists. This is particularly evident in those regions that are capable of capitalising on the proactivity of the food and wine businesses and of introducing experiential and cultural elements into the private and public supply. They thereby advantage themselves of the need increasingly felt by the wineries to bond with customers not simply on the basis of the product itself but also of the drinking experience. This can be done, for example, by means of the architecture and design of the wineries, the exploitation of the surrounding winegrowing landscape, and the organisation of packages that combine hospitality and wellness.

In addition to these sectors that are traditionally included among the creative industries, it will also be interesting to see how the tourist contribution of other areas of creativity – such as digital crafts or the content industry – will evolve in the coming years.

Some examples already exist: from spares for aircraft tables to 3D tourist maps for the visually impaired, to prototypes of personal effects transmissible in file form to hotels to be printed in situ.

Mapping these intersectoral interactions and the supply chain relationships is fundamental from various points of view:

- for a better understanding of the effects of tourism on local economies;

Figure 3   Designer Janne Kyttanen's *Lost Luggage* project (2014) comprises a bag with a complete outfit that can be 3D-printed: so as to travel without luggage or forward it to the destination by email

Source: https://www.youtube.com/watch?v=s5qHF7Kvaik

- for monitoring trends in product and service evolution;
- for identifying support tools for the two sectors that are capable of further stimulating and favouring exchanges and interactions in terms of product development, process innovation and reinforcement of competencies.

Level 3. "Trade follows the films": export strategies and the effects on tourist spending

"Trade follows the films" declared an American slogan from the 1920s, testifying to just how great an impact the lifestyles and consumer goods depicted by the cinema had on American exports. The marriage between tourism and the creative industries can be read in a similar manner. There is no better place today than Italy for realising this. Simply enter the shipping department of any of the great Italian design enterprises in Brianza or Piedmont or of a leading winery in Valpolicella or Chianti: the destination countries indicated on the labels are our great current and wish-list tourism markets. Germany, the Scandinavian countries, China, Russia, Brazil, the United Arab Emirates and South Korea.

The third level of interaction between tourism and the creative industries is therefore to boost tourist expenditure and the development of new tourism markets through the promotion of Made in Italy (or Made in the USA or Made in France) and at the same time promote locally made products thanks to tourism, with the exploitation of the profitable virtuous circle not only of the *place in product*[5] but also of the *product in place*.

Today the challenge facing the tourism and culture worlds (in the broad sense encompassing the creative world) is therefore to explore their relationship on a multiplicity of levels in order to identify the cultural and economic opportunities with a view to integrated exploitation of regions and their products.

These connections are important in terms of tourist expenditure and exports, and of activation of the induced economy and sectoral integration.

This is complex challenge that implies articulated interventions in terms of governance of the territory and of the destinations: it actually involves getting a multiplicity of parties, including tourists, to work with a shared sense of purpose for the creation of new platforms and new contents for enjoying travelling and for constructing highly focussed value networks involving different sectors and different types of actors.

A challenge, finally, that also implies serious reflection as regards the tools required for understanding the market and for the collecting adequate data and statistics because to date tourism expenditure figures are not captured properly in tourism statistics and conventional tourism statistics can offer a misleading view of the contribution tourism makes to economic growth and income.

The ability to better understand the tourism spend and its trends is really fundamental if we are to understand the effects of activating the induced economy and sectoral integration, as well as the effects on exports.

Countless studies are being carried out at national and international level on this last point in order to draft new systems of analysis aimed at a better understanding of the effects of tourist expenditure on national economies and on intersectoral relations for the production of goods and services for tourism.

At national level, some countries including Finland, Australia and Canada, are working on the development of dedicated satellite counts, while at international level the OECD is working on the improvement of tourism expenditure measurement tools in a project for integrating tourism data in the TiVA (Trade in Value Added) database (OECD, 2016).

Notes

[1] See: TEA/AECOM, *2017 Theme Index and Museum Index: The Global Attractions Attendance Report*, TEA, 2018.

[2] See W. Santagata and E. Bertacchini, *Creative Atmosphere: Cultural Industries and Local Development*, 2011, EBLA Working Papers.

[3] Creative Austria is a platform for publicising and communicating the contemporary culture offer in six Austrian destinations (http://www.creativeaustria.at).

[4] Creative Paris is a project launched in 2010 by ADCEP and supported by the Paris Municipality that promotes about 34,000 cultural and creative initiatives and events in the Paris area (http://www.creativeparis.info/en/).

[5] From the title of the famous 2002 article by the American sociologist, Harvey Molotch, who analysed the relationship between the quality of goods and their places of origin.

9   Discovering the Reality and Managing it with Big Data

The rule applies in any sector that there can be no strategy without knowledge of the macro and micro environment you are operating in, and without detailed of familiarity with the characteristics, motivations and needs of your clients.

Having said this, tourism is a difficult sector to map, study and quantify. Official tourist statistics suffer from grave qualitative and quantitative limits and for a long time have not made it possible to obtain a clear picture of the real scale of the phenomenon and of its effects on the economy, even if the investigative tools have been refined over time (one example is the satellite tourism count, see Box 2).

Fundamental figures are often missing from the information available – for example we know very little about how tourists spend their money when they arrive at destination and their real reasons for their trips – and there are information gaps in the estimation/quantification of the black economy. How many tourists are there in second homes? How many tourists are couch-surfing (on whatever basis), or how many are swapping hospitality? And how many are sleeping in homes rented illegally? Furthermore, the available data often arrives late and cannot be used strategically.

Comparing countries is also very difficult as the collection methods vary from country to country, especially as regards international arrivals: in some cases the data are census figures from hospitality establishments and samples taken at the borders in other cases, so that in some states it is the demand that is being monitored and in others the supply.

In international classifications, the numbers recorded for Italy and France refer to border controls (VF: International visitor arrivals at frontiers)

Box 1   Tourism statistics in Italy: the example of cultural tourism

In Italy, according to ISTAT, the national statistics institute, Italian cities of historical and artistic interest are visited by over 43 million tourists every year. This means about 40% of all the arrivals in the peninsula: in terms of arrivals, cultural tourism is therefore the number-one type of tourism in the country. These data are based on counts of arrivals and presences in hospitality establishments and attempt to provide a snapshot of the demand for cultural tourism drawn from information based on an a priori categorisation of the offer, i.e. of the destinations in which the hospitality establishments exist: the data are actually obtained by matching arrivals and presences (broken down according to the foreign state and Italian region of residence of customers) with the holiday locations classified a priori as cities of historical or artistic interest, mountain, lake, seaside, spa, mountain or religious localities, and local capitals and municipalities not otherwise classified, in accordance with the ISTAT classification.

If cultural tourism certainly constitutes a significant portion of the total, it is nevertheless difficult to affirm that arrivals and presences in destinations that are classified as cultural can actually be attributed to this segment: leaving aside Venice and Florence, the top cities of historical and artistic interest in terms of tourist flows include Rome and Milan, for example; but religious tourism is also extremely important in Rome and business travel in Milan. Moreover it is not uncommon for some of the tourists who stay in places of historical and artistic appeal to take little interest in them as they had only chosen to stay in them as they were near their real destination. In fact the link between destination and motivation is not always unequivocal or linear.

As a result, segmenting the demand on the basis of an a priori classification of destinations and reading data from the supply world only, can distort the quantification of what today is the true scale of cultural tourism in the country; this can result on the one hand in failing to include the flows of many minor destinations, and on the other hand from overestimating or underestimating cultural tourist presences in destinations with a mixed vocation.

As regards foreign tourism in Italy – but not domestic travel – the problem can partly be overcome by examining the figures provided by the Bank of Italy which, every quarter, interviews a representative sample of travellers passing through the country's borders: airports, ports, rail and road crossings (inbound-outbound frontier survey).

Such information, drawn directly from the demand side, offers a picture that is perhaps closer to the real one. This is because, unlike the ISTAT figures, it includes the black economy (tourists who stay in second homes, guests of relatives or friends, etc.) and also because it reflects the effective reasons for the trip – the tourists are asked for their own definition – and the tourist spend attributable to them. In this case too, the figures should be read with caution, however, in particular those relating to expenditure because of the limits inherent in the method of collection.

but these figures are compared with those of countries that collect theirs in other ways. Germany (TCE – International tourist arrivals at collective tourism establishments), for example, provides figures on the international tourist arrivals recorded at all hospitality establishments while the Swiss data regard international tourist arrivals recorded at hotels and similar establishments (THS).

Furthermore, even where the collection procedures are the same, some countries include and others exclude certain tourist categories such as, for example, those arriving in ports, citizens resident abroad and so on.

But at least figures for tourist numbers do exist, though with the limits just illustrated. On the other hand, we really know little about the quality of these tourists: how much do they spend? What products do they buy? What services do they look for? How widely do they travel once they have crossed the borders and how to they move through the country?

This is by no means an insignificant limit to our knowledge when, for the development of a locality's tourism, it is decided to focus on quality instead of high numbers, and it is necessary to choose and define the

Box 2   The satellite account

Tourism is a particular phenomenon as it is defined by demand. Visitors purchase various goods and services and one of the principal criticalities from a measurement point of view is specifically the problem of linking their purchases to the total supply of such goods and services inside a given country.
The Tourism Satellite Account (TSA) is a methodology developed by the United Nations to measure the size of economic sectors that are not identified as industries in national accounts, in an attempt to facilitate the qualification of their impact on the economy. Its basic structure is based on the equivalence in an economic datum between the demand for goods and services generated by tourists and the total supply of these goods and services. And so the TSA makes it possible to measure the contribution of tourism to the GDP; the role of tourism compared to that of other economic sectors; the number of jobs generated in an economy by the tourist industries; the tax yield generated by tourist industries; tourist consumption; the impact of tourism on the balance of payments; the characteristics of employment in tourist industries.
However it is a methodologically complex system, and its applicative results – however good – can vary considerably from country to country with great limits, especially in terms of international comparisons of the data.

right products and services and the best strategies for communicating them.

Today, however, all these limits of tourism statistics only regard official figures, those produced by the countries and illustrated by the UNWTO barometers or by Eurostat.

In reality, today there are as many better – much better – figures as could be desired, and we have very high qualities and quantities of data for some types of information. This is because we are in the age of big data which provides an opportunity on everyone's lips, but still exploited by relatively few. But the first steps have actually been taken in the travel industry, among other sectors, as discussed by Viktor Mayer-Schönberger and Kenneth Neil Cukier in their book, *Big data*: in 2003, Oren Etzioni, an American computer science scholar who wanted to obtain a better understanding the swings in airline ticket prices during the days and weeks before a flight, started work on a software application that could process the data on the online offers from airlines and travel sites in real time, in order to examine the link between the prices paid and the moment of purchase. The result was a forecasting model that in 75% of cases was able to let users buy the ticket at the best moment with a considerable savings.

> The model had no understanding of *why*, only *what*. That is, it didn't know any of the variables that go into airline pricing decisions, such as number of seats that remained unsold, seasonality, or wheter some sort of magical Saturday-night-stay might reduce the fare. It based its predictions on what it did know: probabilities gleaned form data about other flights.[1]

The model, named Farecast, was then purchased by Microsoft for $115 million and integrated into the Bing search engine in a section called Bing Travel. Bing Travel does not exist anymore, but the model was adopted by other players such as the Kayak dedicated travel metasearch engine.

Etzioni's analysis is therefore based on processing immense heaps of observations, of big data, so large and multiform as to require new instruments at every stage of the process, from acquisition onwards.

The novelty in this new age did not actually regard the quantity of data (we're talking about terabytes and petabytes all the way to zetabytes), but also the technologies for managing them, as well as their variety, quality and life spans. On one hand, in fact, collection and analysis are no longer possible using traditional software and with single servers, but demand

Figure 1 Purchase simulation on the Kayak metasearch engine

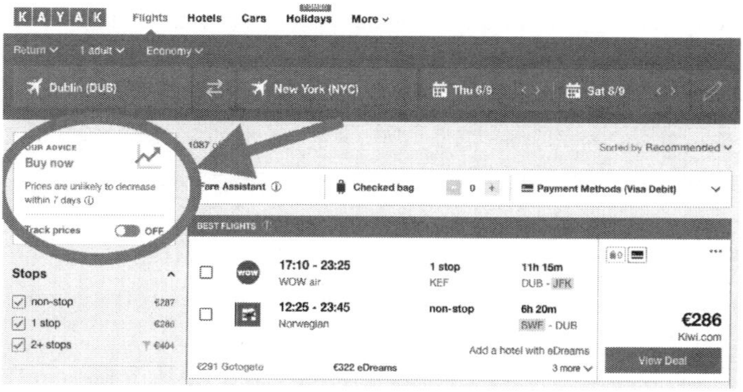

new types of database, new programming languages and new hardware architectures. On the other hand the processed data are, increasingly, non-structured and they barely persist for long enough to perform the necessary analyses. Finally, the other ground-breaking change brought in by the big data era was the partial abandonment of analytical logic processes designed to identify cause–effect relationships.

The big data era challenges the way we live and interact with the world. The most impressive thing is that society must set aside some of its obsessions with cause and effect systems in favour of simple correlations: looking at the *whys*, not just at the *whats*. This upsets centuries of consolidated practice and challenges all our most basic approaches about how to take decisions and understand reality.[2]

The problem therefore is not just methodological but also cultural, and regards the ability to read the obtainable data critically and quantitatively.

Where does this information come from? From the infinite traces that each of us leaves in behavioural terms in social media such as Facebook, Twitter, YouTube or Instagram; in on- and offline transactions (purchases, orders, bookings, shipments), in data transmitted in real time by sensors, files, emails, GPS data, bike- and car-sharing schemes and many others.

As in other economic frameworks, the arrival of big data constitutes a particularly interesting challenge for enterprises and regions in the tourism sector too, and possession of such data and the skills for their interpretation and strategic application inevitably has important implications for the management and promotion of destinations.

The main applications of big data to tourism regard five frameworks in particular: revenue management, the distribution of products and services, managing the trip, financial performance and managing investments.[3]

As regards revenue management, i.e. managing income, the most important opportunities from the application of big data actually relate to pricing policies, particularly delicate for perishable services such as hotel rooms and flights. This is because big data can be input into revenue management algorithms, in order on the one hand to reinforce the development of pricing policies in real time, and also on the other for the inclusion in the analysis of other exogenous factors that influence tourists' decisions – weather forecasts for example. Several important operators in the sector are already moving in this direction, particularly airlines such as British Airways, Air France, KLM, Swiss Airlines or Lufthansa.

Distribution is the other great field of big data application and here we have already seen the first disruptive effects, particularly as regards product personalisation. Table 9.1 exemplifies possible types of personalisation, even if some of them have not yet been tried out concretely.

For the moment the main product personalisation trials have been developed especially by big players in the sector which are able to make considerable investments. These range from Booking.com for the improvement of its recommendation algorithms, to the large hotel chains and to Disney which, in 2013, invested $1 million to develop MyMagic+. This is a system that allows visitors to their parks to plan their visit more effectively and lets Disney follow their movements and spending habits and offer personalised services and prices.

The subject is also of great interest to destinations, and these often do not have the resources financially and in terms of know-how to take advantage of it.

Personalised marketing has its limits and costs however, and consumers could soon get fed up with an excessively customised offer of products that end up by being banal, depriving them of that level of adventurous foreseeability which is an integral part of the travel experience. The big data revolution is certainly an authentic one, but if its efficiency tends to universalise goods and services, brands will have to find new creative ways to compete and differentiate themselves on the market.

The use of big data then also offers significant opportunities on the journey management front, both for businesses and for localities, through

Table 1 Personalisation and big data

Type of personalisation	Example of a targeted proposal
Based on consumption behaviour	We are sorry not to have you on board on the London–Paris flight this week after the pleasure of having you with us in the last six weeks.
Based on social relations	Many of your Facebook friends have visited Krakow in the last two years; so we are offering you a 20% discount to try out this experience for yourself.
Direct, on ancillary consumptions	We know that you enjoyed our restaurant in recent months and we would be pleased to have you with us again this evening, so we are attaching a discount coupon for a free aperitif.
Personalisation based on location	We wish you a pleasant flight to New York. If you are interested in staying for a night at the Hotel Rouge for only €199, we will offer you the transfer by limousine and will be there to meet you on your arrival at the airport.
Personalisation based on inconvenience suffered	We are extremely sorry for the delay in your flight which has probably caused you to miss your connection to Munich: can we book you a first class seat on the next flight at 14.00?

Source: authors on Amadeus, 2013

the study of flows not only from the standpoint of physical movement, but also as regards perception of the experience. Preventing bottlenecks, rescheduling transport in the most efficient manner, minimising flight delays and the associated inconvenience, preventing accidents and programming an efficient use of energy resources are only some of the possible areas of application, and they are also particularly important for localities so as to guarantee sustainable tourism development or for adjusting their promotional policies in real time. Big data actually makes it possible to estimate where the tourist who landed in Zurich in the morning will be in the evening or see how tourists distribute themselves over an area on the basis of their countries of origin, but also foresee and manage flows for special events such as the Olympics, festivals and musical events.

Without doubt a series of questions remain, linked above all to data sensitivity, which have limited or slowed down the use of such information to date.

Certainly among these is the data protection package adopted in May 2016 (General Data Protection Regulation EU 2016/679) that obliges Internet sites to request users' permission to use cookies[4] regarding the services offered and to prepare a register of the processing activities, specifying the reasons for collecting data, the categories of personal data and of interested parties, as well as the security measures implemented, for transparency purposes and for compliance with the right of access to the data by users.

This gives users more power to limit the collection of information on their online behaviour that could be used for generating sales strategies, but at the same time it sometimes impedes their use of the site's most interesting functions which cannot be activated without explicit approval of the use of profiling cookies.

Also unresolved is the broad topic of access and efficient integration between various sources for effective data management, for example between operators in the same sector or belonging to the same supply chain.

As regards this last front, interesting experiments are in progress for the application of blockchain technology to make data accessible to all the participating parties in a given chain without the possibility of error and data corruption, especially in aviation where the problem of integrating the flight data sources is particularly appreciated and critical.

An interesting example comes from the project developed by a team comprising British Airways, Heathrow Airport, Geneva Airport, Miami International Airport and SITA Lab to explore if and how blockchain technology can help to create a "single source of truth" for flight data. This through the creation of an Aviation Blockchain Sandbox, a platform that will permit the development of applications based on distributed ledgers.

Notes

[1] V. Mayer-Schönberger and K. Cukier, *Big Data: A Revolution that Will Transform how We Live, Work, and Think*, Boston, Houghton Mifflin Harcourt, 2013, p. 5.

[2] Ibid.

[3] T.H. Davenport, *At the Big Data Crossroads: Turning Towards a Smarter Travel Experience*, Amadeus, 2013.

[4] Cookies are little data files associated with specific website pages that make it possible to obtain information for improving the use of web functions but also to profile users on the basis of their specific characteristics, not simply their personal details, but also on their online navigation experience, on the type of pages visited, on the products purchased, etc. Each of these pieces of information, useful for navigation or for statistical purposes is read every time the user visits, and processed to obtain an identikit. The cookies are then destroyed or renewed depending on how they have been set by the website proprietors.

10 Wars, Epidemics, Conflicts and the World to Come

Looking on tourism as an experimental laboratory and an opportunity for economic and social development is indisputably fascinating, with all the pertinent ifs and buts, vis-à-vis the various areas of sustainability (there are so many themes that we have not discussed in this book, from sexual tourism to the devastation of landscapes triggered by the development of tourism infrastructures), and we cannot be indifferent to the prospects of development of the sector.

To what extent the positive UNWTO growth forecasts will be confirmed and where this development will really be concentrated also depends today on a great unknown: international conflicts and the rise and geographical diffusion of Islamic terrorism, the political fortunes of the Middle Eastern and North African countries (MENA).

1. Terrorism, wars, natural disasters and geopolitical crises

In general, tourism is quite resilient to political and economic crises, to outrages and natural disasters. Looking at the past, in fact, at macro level these events have almost never halted tourist flows, which were simply redistributed differently at world level: if the Red Sea became dangerous, tourists changed direction towards the coasts of Italy, Croatia or Spain.

The only real pause (and a fairly short one) in the last 20 years occurred as a result of the 2008 financial crisis and the consequent recession that led to a sharp fall in international arrivals in 2009. This crisis was a profound one, deemed by some to be the worst since the days of the Great Depression, but tourism was already beginning to grow again in 2010.

At micro level on the other hand, the consequences of acts of terrorism or health emergencies are certainly felt more and, even if the duration of these effects can differ widely depending on the places in which the events occur geographically and their type, in general tourism tends to forget its crises in a hurry and quickly resumes its normal growth patterns.

Nevertheless, the tourists' memory has always worked at two speeds. In the West, in the USA and, in general, in the developed countries, the effects have historically been more often short-lived; this is shown in recent times by the attacks at the Madrid stations in 2004 (191 dead and over 2,000 injured) and by the 2005 attack on London's public transport system (56 dead and 700 injured) or, in other ways, by the Fukushima Daiichi 2011 nuclear disaster.

This last case is a particularly good example: on 11 March 2011 a magnitude 9 earthquake and the powerful tsunami that followed it devastated north-east Japan, triggering the meltdown of the three reactors in the Tepco plant at Daiichi in the worst nuclear disaster since Chernobyl.

The balance was appalling in terms of human lives, devastation and long-term and far-ranging environmental effects because of the radioactive contamination. Nevertheless, the fall in international arrivals in Japan lasted just one year and there were already 2 million more tourists in 2013 than in 2010.

The consequences for tourism of the 2004 Madrid train attacks were resolved in just a few weeks and the London bombs the following year had virtually no effects on flows of tourists.

The political and economic stability of these countries, their brand as destinations, their weight in international politics and their economic resources and know-how at national level, but also in their business fabric, made it easier to manage these crises.

On the other hand, in countries that are already the theatre of clashes, even if only territorially limited and isolated, the sustainability and opening of tourism are much less resilient than peaceful countries to deteriorations, however slight, in conflicts and violence.

The vigour and permanence on tourism of malevolent events such as terrorist attacks or natural disasters do not depend on geography only but also on the type. Epidemics such as Severe Acute Respiratory Syndrome (SARS) in China in 2002/2003 or Ebola haemorrhagic fever in West Africa in 2014 evidently require their own natural resolutory times, as do the reorganisation of the tourism offer after catastrophes such as the 2010 earthquake in Haiti or the 2004 tsunami in Indonesia, Sri Lanka and Thailand, just to mention a few of those of greatest significance from a tourist standpoint. Terrorism on the other hand is imponderable and aleatory. It happens and provokes its effects, but then it is impossible to know what the next target might be and people react as a consequence: if there are no repeats of the attacks, they forget and begin making normal plans again.

The effects of terrorism actually last less than those of other events. According to the World Travel and Tourism Council (WTTC) 13 months are required on average for recovery from a terrorist attack while up to 27 months are required for political crises.

Box 1   Tourism and the Arab Spring

The waves of protests and revolutions from 2010 onwards in the MENA nations have profoundly affected incoming tourism in these regions.
The effects have been particularly grave for two countries heavily committed to tourism, Egypt and Tunisia, for which the GDP contribution to GDP amounts respectively to about 11% and 12%.
Both Egypt and Tunisia initially experienced a fall in arrivals following the events of the aforesaid Arab Spring and then, after a slight recovery, growth was stymied again following the terrorist attacks in 2015 and 2016.

Figure 1   International tourist arrivals in Egypt, Tunisia and Syria

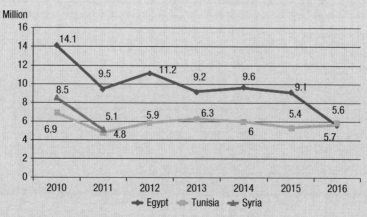

Source: Elaborated from UNWTO 2016 data

In 2015 and in 2016, following the 2015 attacks in Tunis (Bardo Museum) and on the beach at Sousse, Tunisia suffered a total collapse in arrivals from Europe, and from the UK in particular as many of the victims were British. The country tried to react by targeting other markets such as Russia, and with an international 12-language advertising campaign (#True Tunisia) – particularly intense in the top European capitals – that included a 15-episode web series that illustrated the marvels of the country. Furthermore, the country has worked hard to strengthen security measures and controls.

These strategies, while being considerably successful at the moment, have been unable to counterbalance the harm, and the recovery of tourism in Tunisia requires deeper reflection which must also be extended to the very structure of the sector and its rules, in particular those regarding the labour market.

Tunisia's socio-economic conditions and the instability stemming from it are deep-rooted and also involve an insufficiently productive and inclusive economy, that is highly uneven territorially, in which tourism is a part and partial cause. The activities linked to the sector are in fact almost exclusively concentrated on the coasts and are characterised by mass tourism services whose competitiveness depends considerably on containing costs: these weigh above all on a labour force that is forced to move about continually, in conditions of wage volatility, precariousness and the substantial absence of safeguards.

Moreover, the Tunisian model is highly dependent on foreign demand, with no real development strategy for the domestic market that would not only develop the coastal areas for internal tourists but also the regions of the interior.

Figure 2   An image of the #True Tunisia *campaign featuring Sousse and the Roman ruins at El Jem, among the most important in Africa.*

Egypt has also followed a substantially similar route; international arrivals were 30% down after the 2011 revolution and a weak recovery that was always threatened by the effects of terrorist attacks that have followed numerously one after another since then, including the Airbus from Sharm-el-Sheik that was shot down in 2015, the bus of tourists assaulted in Cairo and the attack on a resort in Hurghada in 2016. Finally, even more devastating were the effects on Syria where the florid tourist economy was another victim of the civil war. UNWTO figures on the sector stop at 2010, but in a 2013 interview with the broadcaster, Al Arabyia, the Syrian Minister for Tourism, Bishr Riad Yaziji, had declared that following the outbreak of the conflict in March 2011 the tourism industry had lost $1.5 billion with a 94% fall in revenues from 2011 to 2013, damage to almost 300 tourist establishments and the devastation of important archaeological sites, artistic assets and historic towns such as Aleppo. Before the onset of the conflict, tourism revenues constituted 12% of Syria's GDP and the sector employed about 11% of the country's workers.

Source: Al Arabyia, 2013.

Moreover, it is interesting to note that only a minimum part the outcome of terrorist attacks depends on their magnitude: the impacts of the bombs in Indonesia in 2002 and 2005 were quite different in terms of loss of life but fairly similar in terms of fallout on tourism.

2.   The new targets of Islamic terrorism

Between 2001 and 2016 tourism and transport were hit by terrorism 366 times with attacks in 58 countries and 8 regions of the world,[1] highlighting just how much tourism and places of recreation have become terrorism's preferred *soft targets*.

The killing of foreign tourists opens up media coverage to their countries of origin and is a low-cost tool for conveying the most extensive ideological message of political opposition. As they are open to everyone, hotels, restaurants, pubs, theatres and private properties with public areas, are vulnerable to attacks as the probabilities of failure are low. Moreover, terrorists want to strike at lifestyle, a tradition of Western modernity which has organised working hours, weekends, holidays and trips along a historical path linked to industrialisation, to social status with paid holidays and vacations, to the values of freedom to choose and to amuse oneself however one wants, without religious or political diktat.[2]

For terrorists, tourism therefore constitutes a target which allows them to strike at least three of the enemy's nerve centres: communications, lifestyle and the economy.

As regards communications, the attacks on Western tourists have attracted much more attention from the international media than those on other targets, thereby providing terrorists and their actions with the greatest visibility worldwide and amplifying the destructive fallout for local economies and the perception of the locations.

Terrorism also strikes peoples' lifestyle on at least two levels: freedom to travel without fear, on the one hand, and dialogue between the tourists and the host community on the other.

Whether relating to the attacks occur in Europe or elsewhere, the first victim is the sense of security that is naturally inherent in an activity which is supposed to be relaxing and fun, when defences are lowered in order to welcome new experiences. Terrorism creates a state of permanent alertness to which tourists are not accustomed but with which they will have to live constantly in future years, not only as individuals, but also as members of multi-ethnic communities (management of fear where you live) and as citizens of a political and economic space (greater limits on people's mobility resulting from border security management measures).

There is however another level of the life and coexistence of individuals and groups which is modified by terrorism: the relationship between tourists and host communities, in particular when tourists are attacked in the countries of origin of the terrorist groups.

If it is true, as maintained by the United Nations or by the WTTC,[3] that tourism can be seen as a tool for intercultural dialogue between the West and moderate Islam – the part that is open and willing to mediate to accept "the secular values of commercialised hospitality, of sports activities and tourist travel"[4] – terrorism shatters this common space, by repelling tourists while morally and economically punishing those who welcome them.

In addition to all this are the consequences for the targeted countries and for the operators in the sector. These can obviously be direct and limited to lost income resulting from reduced tourist flows, to costs borne for handling emergencies, to repatriations, to reimbursements or to losses on the stock markets. But they are also indirect, for instance, lower investments and foreign currency reserves, increased transaction costs, unemployment and, in general, a deterioration of the real economy that can also translate into a recession, transforming itself into a society-wide scourge and fertile ground for extremism and terrorism. The harm obviously varies from country to country, depending on the weight on the local tourism economy in terms of gross domestic product. For Tunisia, for example, striking tourism is the equivalent of striking the petroleum sector in Algeria or Libya.

What can be expected?

Predicting what we might expect in the coming years as regards the terrorism/tourism relationship is really difficult.

There can be no doubt that countries like Turkey, Egypt and Tunisia are suffering its extreme consequences, and so too are Algeria, Libya, Jordan and the entire MENA area in general. The front is also extending then to several South-East Asian nations as can be seen from the attacks in Indonesia and Thailand.

More complicated, however, is understanding how terrorism will affect tourism in Europe. The Mediterranean countries of the EU are actually benefitting considerably from the crises in the Middle East and North Africa, as their resorts and cities of art attract all those tourists who are frightened by the escalation of attacks in tourist localities in North Africa and the Red Sea.

The first challenge for Europe and, in particular, for countries like Portugal, Spain, Italy and Croatia, will therefore be to consolidate the positive economic effects and make it structural.

However Europe itself is a target for attacks and the main fronts are France and Germany, two central players for the competitiveness of the continent's tourism.

However, in a global market that no longer thinks in terms of destinations but of macro areas and continents, the new hazardousness perceived in these two countries cannot be constrained within their boundaries but ends up afflicting the European system as a whole. If there are further attacks, how will the Americans look on transatlantic travel? Will the new tourists from Asia feel that it is safe to undertake a tour in Central Europe? And how will it be possible to protect brand "Europe" whatever the consequences of terrorist attacks really are? The questions are obviously also linked to the theme of the media and information. The latter should be targeted as far as possible on security and preventive measures for tourists and residents alike, while avoiding alarmism which may also be guided by the same vested economic interests that are already fomenting further tensions and disputes between countries.

In general, these questions concern international tourism but evidently also intra-area travel, that of Europeans inside Europe.

Finally, it is necessary to mention the fact that Europe and its coasts, and those of Italy and Greece above all, are the landing points for hundreds of thousands of migrants fleeing from wars and seeking better lives: 1 million in 2015 according to the International Organization for Migration (IOM).

This has reflections for tourism on at least two fronts. The first is that the landing points and the tourism localities often overlap, i.e. the coasts, resulting in problems in terms of attractiveness and of joint management of the needs of the various populations, migrants, residents and tourists.

And secondly, the migration flows sharpen the needs for border controls and additional security measures which inevitably end up affecting tourists.

It is therefore particularly difficult to forecast the outcome of this mix of factors that generate opposite or at least contrasting effects.

It is simpler, however, to look at the micro level, at the world of small businesses and operators in the sector who will need to implement or reinforce their risk prevention and management strategies in the coming years.

Notes

[1] Source: Itstime, 2016.

[2] N. Costa, *Turismo e terrorismo jihadista*, Rubbettino, Soveria Mannelli, 2016, p. 60.

[3] In 2016 the WTTC dedicated a report to this theme, entitled *Tourism as a Driver for Peace*.

[4] *Ibid.*, p. 11.

11 Conclusions. Destination: Sustainability

As we have been in the previous chapters, tourism is a sector in extraordinary expansion and rapid innovation. It is an incredible economic and employment resource, it provides an opportunity for development that is relatively accessible for a huge variety of places, allows different peoples to get to know each other and opens up a huge employment market.

The enormous growth of the tourism industry and of tourism in recent decades has also made it essential to reflect on the sustainability of these trends in the medium term and on the negative effects that tourism is having in many places around the globe.

However, some destinations have already exceeded their carrying capacity,[1] i.e. the index that indicates the limit beyond which the pathological aspects of tourism are manifested: in the social, environmental and economic fields; even political. From that moment the damages caused by tourism exceed the benefits, deeply affecting the physical and cultural identity of the places, and eroding and consuming the natural, artistic and social resources of the community.

Water, energy, monuments, beaches, streets, perfumes and landscapes are increasingly subject to multiple uses by different groups of consumers – residents, tourists, hikers or tourism enterprises – whose employment modalities are often in competition with one another, if not indeed in conflict: the resources in question are not renewable so the irreversibility of some processes can constitute a total collapse of the identifying and economic value of the locations.

The difficulty inherent in the management of these resources is also that the exclusion of individuals or groups from enjoying them could be found to be socially unacceptable or simply impossible on a technical level.

New bigger and bigger aircraft, gigantic ports under construction, millions of cars on the roads heading for holiday resorts, millions of cubic metres of new hotel buildings, private houses placed on the tourism market, and millions of people from the most varied regions of the Earth visiting tiny destinations of a few hundred inhabitants of whose customs and history they know little or nothing.

What effect does this have on local economies and on the future development of the sector? And what measures can we take not only to guarantee tourism's sustainability, minimising the environmental and social consequences of tourism development, but also to guarantee sustainable local development through tourism?

In recent years the over-tourism phenomenon has achieved great media prominence and pictures of Venetian bridges groaning under the weight of tourists, bunches of people squashed together to take selfies in front of the *Mona Lisa* or the protests of Barcelona residents against tourists have gone around the world on newspapers and magazine covers. But such sensationalist images risk creating a simplistic image of a multifaceted and highly complex problem.

In reality the topic is a very delicate one: the positive and negative effects of the development of tourism are tightly interwoven and difficult to isolate, given that they manifest themselves on different levels – environmental, economic and social – and on different geographical scales, and relate to different stakeholder groups.

For this reason, when it comes to making rules for it, forecasts and so on, it is fundamental for this to be done in a horizontal manner.

Unlike many other sectors, tourism is actually not sustainable within a perimeter that identifies it as a well-defined unit, as in reality it is pervasive and transversal. Tourism embraces the environment but also agriculture, cultural heritage, infrastructures, exports and the economy: tourism embraces everything. And so do its negative effects when tourist pressure on destinations becomes too high. A particularly representative example of these complex intersections is that of Venice:

> the historic centre of the city counts about 54,000 inhabitants while the "official" statistics tell us that there are about 10 million presences per year but estimates indicate at least 25. The costs of this pressure can be seen on two fronts: just to give one example, the multiplication of the costs of waste collection and management – about an extra €30 million every year[2] – which is still manual in the historic centre

Figure 1   The Venice Syndrome (2012)

Source: Andreas Pichler on the effects of tourism on the city of Venice

as this is one of the most extensive pedestrian zones in Europe. Considering the plastic waste only, if each tourist in the city consumed just one bottle of water this would amount to 25 million plastic bottles rapidly filling the rubbish bins of the city's historic centre every year. And waste, of course, is only one of the high costs paid by Venice's fragile and unique ecosystem as a result of its touristic success.

The cost–effect relationship between environmental costs and tourist pressure is not always so evident however. Some effects are more hidden and only reveal themselves in the medium to long terms and in geographical areas that may be quite far apart.

For some destinations to count on tourism entails enormous property development and exponential growth in the construction sector. In order to build houses, hotels and roads involves the use of millions of cubic metres of cement which, in turn require millions of tonnes of sand: a scarce and fundamental resource in many sectors, which is sourced nowadays by dredging from the seas, with turnovers of billions and with devastating effects on the environment, from erosion of the coasts to the disappearance of entire portions of islands and dry land.

For the sole colossal Palm Islands and Palm Jumeirah project alone, Dubai dredged 150 million tonnes of sand from its own sea beds.[3] And the Palm Islands are only a minimal part of what was a gigantic building development of a city intended to become a must on the tourist bucket list of international travellers.

The consequences of tourism are not only environmental, of course, but also have important economic, social and cultural effects for the local communities in destinations, old and new.

Imbalances in real estate revenues, in the rental market and the consequent crowding out of local inhabitants, triggered by the enormous expansion of short rentals and of the Airbnb model, are creating great problems in the historic centres of European cities and spurring administrators and governments all over the world to assess new and stricter regulatory systems. Other destinations are struggling so as not to lose their identifying values and the traditions swallowed up by the consolidation of touristic mono-economies.

The containment of "negative tourism", that of large numbers, excessive seasonal concentration, low quality and low economic interest in the style of consumption, can only be managed through long and complex strategic planning work that does not only affect the tourism sector but the whole territory: from urban planning to the choice of industrial and productive vocations of the territory, from cultural policies to social and housing ones. Too often the problems of over-tourism have been addressed by focussing only on the tourism phenomenon.

Higher taxes, dispersion tactics, restrictions to rentals and lodging limitations can at best constitute a local buffer to a problem which needs to be tackled on a much broader scale, with the promotion of information and awareness among tourists, first of all, and among residents and operators; sustaining the development of diversified economies also facilitating the establishment of research and training centers; developing attractive housing policies for residents; incentivising the transition to climate resilient and energy-efficient investments[4]; promoting efficient use of bed taxes; exploiting the enormous potentials that derive from ICT for monitoring and forecasting flows; investing in smart tools (destination cards, intelligent signage, etc.) in order to facilitate improved fruition of the territory and historic centres.

These are the challenges that tourism must tackle urgently in order to continue to be one of the strong sectors of the global economy.

Notes

[1] According to the UNWTO, carrying capacity can be defined as the maximum number of people that may visit a tourist destination at the same time, without causing destruction of the physical, economic and sociocultural environment and an unacceptable decrease in the quality of visitors' satisfaction.

[2] Figures from the Venice Municipality, 2017.

[3] This theme is the subject of Denis Delestrac's "Sand Wars" documentary (2015).

[4] For greater information on investments and financing for sustainable tourism see OECD, *Tourism Trends and Policies 2018*, OECD Publishing, Paris, 2018, pp. 93–120.

Bibliography

Boatto ,V. and Gennari A.J. (2011), *La roadmap del turismo enologico*, Franco Angeli, Milan.

Butler, R. W. and Russell, R. (2010), *Giants of Tourism*, CABI.

Capeci, F. (2018), *Post Millennial Marketing: The Biggest Change in Marketing Ever, Led by New Generations. If We Allow Them to Drive it.*

Catucci, S. (2013), *Imparare dalla Luna*, Quodlibet, Macerata.

Cohen, E. (2017). The paradoxes of space tourism. *Tourism Recreation Research*, 42(1), 22–31.

Costa, N. (2016), *Turismo e terrorismo jihadista*, Rubbettino, Soveria Mannelli.

Creaton, S. (2014), *Ryanair. How a Small Irish Airline Conquered Europe*, Aurum Press Limited.

Eberstadt, N. and Groth, H. (2007). *Europe's Coming Demographic Challenge: Unlocking the Value of Health.* AEI Press.

Johnson, M. R. and Martin, D. (2016). The anticipated futures of space tourism, *Mobilities*, 11(1), 135–151.

Marr, B. (2016), *Big Data in Practice: How 45 Succesful Companies Used Big Data Anytics to Deliver Extraordinary Results*, Wiley.

Mayer-Schönberger V. and Cukier, K. (2013), *Big Data: A Revolution that Will Transform how We Live, Work, and Think*, Boston, Houghton Mifflin Harcourt.

McKinsey&Company/WTTC (2017), *Coping with Success. Managing Overcrowding in Tourism Destinations*, online at https://www.wttc.org/-/media/files/reports/policy-research/coping-with-success---managing-overcrowding-in-tourism-destinations-2017.pdf.

Molotch, H. (2002), Place in product, *International Journal of Urban and Regional Research* 26(4), 665–88.

OECD (2014), *Tourism and the Creative Economy, OECD Studies on Tourism*, Paris, OECD Publishing.

OECD (2016), *OECD Tourism Trends and Policies 2016*, Paris, OECD Publishing.

OECD (2018), *OECD Tourism Trends and Policies 2018*, Paris, OECD Publishing.

Pine, B. J. and Gilmore J.H. (1999), *The Experience Economy: Work is Theatre &* *Every Business a Stage*, Boston, Harvard Business Press.

Santagata, W. (2010), *The Culture Factory. Creativity and the Production of Culture*, Springer.

Segreto, L., Manera, C. and Pohl, M. (2009), *Europe at the Seaside: The Economic History of Mass Tourism in the Mediterranean*, New York, Berghahn Books.

Stone, B. (2017), *The Upstarts. Uber, Airbnb and the Battle for the New Silicon Valley*, Penguin.

Urry, J. (1990), *The Tourist Gaze: Leisure and Travel in Contemporary Societies* (published in association with *Theory, Culture and Society*), London Sage.

Wharton, E. (1908), *A Motor-Flight through France*, Scribner.

Zuelow, E. (2015), *A History of Modern Tourism*, Macmillan International Higher Education.